Guide to the Bodhisattva's Way of Life

Suggested study or reading order for beginners of books by Venerable Geshe Kelsang Gyatso Rinpoche

SHANTIDEVA'S

Guide to the Bodhisattva's Way of Life

HOW TO ENJOY A LIFE OF GREAT MEANING AND ALTRUISM

Originally translated and revised from Sanskrit into Tibetan by several translators, including Dharmashribhadra, Rinchen Sangpo, Shakyamati, Sumatikirti and Loden Sherab.

This present translation from Tibetan into English was rendered by Gen-la Kelsang Thubten under the compassionate guidance of Venerable Geshe Kelsang Gyatso Rinpoche.

THARPA PUBLICATIONS
UK • US • CANADA
AUSTRALIA • ASIA

First edition 2002 – 5 Impressions
Second edition 2018 - Impression 2 (2021)

Tharpa Publications UK
Conishead Priory
Ulverston, Cumbria
LA12 9QQ, England

Tharpa Publications US
47 Sweeney Road
Glen Spey, NY 12737
USA

Tharpa Publications has offices around the world,
and Tharpa books are published in most major languages.
See page 239 for contact details.

Chapter illustrations by Mr. Chew Choon.
Cover painting by Ms. Belinda Ho.
Front-flap painting of the Bodhisattva Shantideva.

Library of Congress Control Number: 2002114543

British Library Cataloguing in Publication Data
A catalogue record for this book is
available from the British Library.

ISBN 978-1-910368-74-9 – paperback
ISBN 978-1-910368-75-6 – ePub
ISBN 978-1-910368-76-3 – Kindle

Set in Palatino by Tharpa Publications
Printed and bound by CPI Group (UK) Ltd.

Paper supplied from well-managed forests and other controlled
sources, and certified in accordance with the rules of the
Forest Stewardship Council.

Contents

Introduction

The Buddhist masterpiece called *Guide to the Bodhisattva's Way of Life* was composed by Bodhisattva Shantideva, a great Buddhist Master who lived in the eighth century CE. This holy scripture is a very practical guide that teaches us how to enter, make progress on, and complete the Buddhist path to enlightenment. It is a condensation of all Buddha's teachings and it shows clearly how these teachings can be integrated into our daily life.

Shantideva's *Guide* has been the inspiration of many great spiritual works, such as *Eight Verses of Training the Mind* by the great Kadampa Teacher Langri Tangpa, and *Training the Mind in Seven Points* by Bodhisattva Chekhawa. Both these texts explain how to cherish others, equalize self and others, and exchange self with others, how to practise 'taking and giving', and how to transform adverse conditions into methods for attaining liberation. All these teachings are extracted from Shantideva's *Guide*. Many Kadampa practitioners keep Shantideva's teachings in their hearts, and Je Tsongkhapa and his disciples greatly praised Shantideva's work.

Through studying many Buddhist texts we may become a renowned scholar; but, if we do not put Buddha's teachings – the Dharma – into practice, our understanding of Buddhism will remain hollow, with no power to solve our own or others' problems. Expecting intellectual understanding of

Dharma alone to solve our problems is like a sick person hoping to cure his or her illness through merely reading medical instructions without actually taking the medicine. As Shantideva says in the fifth chapter:

(109)   We need to put Buddha's teachings, the Dharma,
            into practice
        Because nothing can be accomplished just by
            reading words.
        A sick man will never be cured of his illness
        Through merely reading medical instructions!

Each and every living being has the sincere wish to avoid permanently all suffering and problems. We normally try to do this by using external methods, but no matter how successful we are from a worldly point of view – no matter how materially wealthy, powerful or highly respected we become – we will never find permanent liberation from suffering and problems. Suffering, pain, unhappiness and problems do not exist outside the mind. They are unpleasant feelings, and feelings are types of mind. Only by transforming our mind can we eliminate suffering and problems permanently. The method for doing this is explained clearly in Shantideva's *Guide*.

In reality, all the problems we experience day to day come from our self-cherishing and self-grasping – misconceptions that exaggerate our own importance. However, because we do not understand this, we normally blame others for our problems, and this just makes them worse. From these two basic misconceptions arise all our other delusions, such as anger and attachment, causing us to experience endless problems. We can solve all of these problems by sincerely practising the instructions presented in this book. At least we should memorize from each chapter those verses we find most helpful, and contemplate their meaning again and again until our mind becomes peaceful and positive. We should then try to maintain this peaceful state of mind day and night without interruption. By doing this, we will experience a happy and meaningful life.

We should read this book with a happy mind, free from distraction and negative views. It is also very important to improve our understanding of *Guide to the Bodhisattva's Way of Life* by studying commentaries such as *Meaningful to Behold*. Through sincerely practising these instructions we can transform our ordinary, self-centred intentions into the supreme good heart, our ordinary, confused view into profound wisdom, and our ordinary way of life into a Bodhisattva's way of life. In this way, we will attain the supreme inner peace of enlightenment, which is the real meaning of our human life.

Geshe Kelsang Gyatso,
USA,
April 2002.

In Sanskrit:

Bodhisattvacharyavatara

In Tibetan:

Jang chub sem pai cho pa la jug pa

In English:

Guide to the Bodhisattva's Way of Life

Chapter 1:

An Explanation of the

Benefits of Bodhichitta

Whereas all other virtues are like plantain trees,
In that they are exhausted once they bear fruit,
The enduring celestial tree of bodhichitta
Is not exhausted but increases by bearing fruit.

An Explanation of the Benefits of Bodhichitta

Homage to the enlightened Buddhas and Bodhisattvas.

(1)   I prostrate to the enlightened Buddhas endowed
            with the Truth Body,
        And to the Bodhisattvas and all other objects of
            prostration.
        I will explain briefly, in accordance with the
            Scriptures,
        How to engage in the condensed practices of the
            Bodhisattva.

(2)   There is nothing written here that has not been
            explained before,
        And I have no special skills in composition.
        My reason for writing this is to benefit others
        And to keep my mind acquainted.

(3) Thus, the strength of my faith and my virtuous
    realizations
    Might for a while be increased by this,
    And perhaps others who are as fortunate as I
    Might also find this meaningful to behold.

(4) This precious human life, so hard to find,
    Offers the ultimate goal for living beings.
    If we do not strive to accomplish this goal now,
    How will such a precious opportunity arise again?

(5) Just as on a dark and cloudy night
    A flash of lightning for a moment illuminates all,
    So for the worldly, through the power of Buddha's
    blessings,
    A virtuous intention occasionally and briefly occurs.

(6) Thus, while our virtues are mostly weak,
    Our non-virtues are extremely strong and fearsome.
    Other than bodhichitta – a compassionate mind
    wishing for enlightenment –
    What virtue can overcome the heaviest evils?

(7) The Able Ones, the Buddhas, who have considered
    this for many aeons,
    Have all seen bodhichitta to be the most beneficial
    Because, through it, countless masses of living
    beings
    Can easily attain the supreme bliss of enlightenment.

(8) Those who wish to destroy their own suffering,
    Those who wish to dispel the suffering of others,
    And those who wish to experience much happiness
    Should never forsake the practice of bodhichitta.

(9)   The moment bodhichitta is generated
Even in pitiful beings bound within the prison of
    samsara,
They become Bodhisattvas – a 'Son or Daughter of
    Buddha' –
And are worthy of veneration by humans and
    worldly gods.

(10)   Just like the supreme elixir that transmutes into gold,
Bodhichitta can transform this impure body we
    have taken
Into the priceless jewel of a Buddha's form.
Therefore, firmly maintain bodhichitta.

(11)   Since the limitless wisdom of Buddha, the Sole
    Navigator of living beings,
Upon thorough investigation has seen its
    preciousness,
Those who wish to be free from samsara's suffering
Should firmly maintain this precious mind of
    bodhichitta.

(12)   Whereas all other virtues are like plantain trees,
In that they are exhausted once they bear fruit,
The enduring celestial tree of bodhichitta
Is not exhausted but increases by bearing fruit.

(13)   Just as when those who are greatly afraid rely upon
    a courageous one,
Whoever relies upon bodhichitta will immediately
    be freed from danger
Even if they have committed unbearable evils;
So why do the conscientious not rely upon it?

(14)   Just like the fire at the end of the aeon,
        In an instant it completely consumes all great evil.
        Its countless benefits were explained by the wise
            Protector Maitreya
        To Bodhisattva Sudhana.

(15)   In brief, you should know
        That bodhichitta has two types:
        The mind that observes enlightenment and aspires,
        And the mind that observes enlightenment and
            engages.

(16)   Just as the distinction between wishing to go
        And actually going is understood,
        So, respectively, the wise should understand
        The difference between these two bodhichittas.

(17)   From the mind that aspires to enlightenment,
        Great effects arise while in samsara;
        But an uninterrupted flow of good fortune does
            not ensue
        As it does from the engaging mind.

(18)   For whoever takes up the engaging mind of
            bodhichitta
        With the intention never to turn back
        From completely liberating
        The infinite living beings throughout all realms,

(19)   From that time forth, for him there will arise –
        Even if he is asleep or apparently unconcerned –
        Vast and powerful merit, equal to space,
        That flows without interruption.

(20)   For the sake of those with lesser inclinations,
        These benefits were explained with logical reasons
        By the Tathagata himself
        In *Sutra Requested by Subahu*.

(21)   If even the thought to relieve
        The headaches of others
        Is a beneficial intention
        That results in infinite merit,

(22)   What can be said of the wish
        To dispel the immeasurable misery
        Of each and every living being
        And lead them all to countless good qualities?

(23)   Does our father or mother
        Have such a beneficial intention as this?
        Do the gods or the sages?
        Does even Brahma himself?

(24)   If, before generating bodhichitta, these living
            beings
        Do not even dream of such a mind
        For their own sakes,
        How will they develop it for the sake of others?

(25)   This mind to benefit living beings,
        Which does not arise in others even for their own
            sakes,
        Is an extraordinary jewel of a mind,
        Whose birth is an unprecedented wonder.

(26) How can we possibly measure
The benefits of this jewel of a mind –
The source of joy for all living beings
And the cure for all their sufferings?

(27) If the mere intention to benefit others
Is more meritorious than making offerings to the
    Buddhas,
What can be said of actually striving
For the happiness of every single living being?

(28) Although living beings wish to be free from
    suffering,
They run straight towards the causes of suffering;
And although they wish for happiness,
Out of ignorance they destroy it like a foe.

(29) For those who are deprived of happiness
And afflicted with many sorrows,
Bodhichitta bestows upon them boundless joy,
Eradicates all their suffering,

(30) And even dispels their confusion.
Where is there virtue equal to this?
Where is there even such a friend?
Where is there merit such as this?

(31) If even someone who repays a kindness
Is worthy of some praise,
What can be said of the Bodhisattva who helps
    others
Regardless of whether or not they help him?

(32)   If someone regularly, or even just once,
        Gives food in a disdainful manner,
        Which satisfies a few beings for only half a day,
        People honour him or her as virtuous;

(33)   So what can be said of one who eternally gives
        To countless living beings
        The everlasting, unsurpassed bliss of the Sugatas,
        Fulfilling all their wishes?

(34)   Buddha said that whoever generates an evil mind
        Towards a Bodhisattva, a supreme benefactor,
        Will remain in hell for as many aeons
        As the moments for which that evil mind was
            generated;

(35)   But, for whoever generates a pure mind of faith,
        The effects of good fortune will increase even more
            than that.
        Even when Bodhisattvas are faced with great
            adversity,
        Negativity does not arise; rather, their virtues
            naturally increase.

(36)   I prostrate to those who have generated
        The holy, precious mind of bodhichitta;
        And I go for refuge to those sources of happiness
        Who bestow bliss even upon those who harm
            them.

This concludes the first chapter of *Guide to the Bodhisattva's Way of Life*, entitled 'An Explanation of the Benefits of Bodhichitta'.

Chapter 2:

Purifying Negativity

To maintain this precious mind of bodhichitta,
I make excellent offerings ...
Lakes and pools adorned with lotuses,
And the beautiful call of wild geese;

CHAPTER 2

Purifying Negativity

(1)   To maintain this precious mind of bodhichitta,
I make excellent offerings to the oceans of good
    qualities –
The Buddhas, the stainless jewel of the holy
    Dharma,
And the assembly of Bodhisattvas.

(2)   However many flowers and fruits there are,
And all the different types of medicine;
All the jewels there are in the world,
And all the pure, refreshing waters;

(3)   Mountains of jewels, forest groves,
And quiet and joyful places;
Heavenly trees adorned with flowers,
And trees whose branches hang with delicious
    fruits;

(4)   Scents that come from the celestial realms,
Incense, wish-granting trees and jewelled trees;
Harvests that need no cultivation,
And all ornaments that are suitable to be offered;

(5)   Lakes and pools adorned with lotuses,
And the beautiful call of wild geese;
Everything that is unowned
Throughout all worlds as extensive as space –

(6)   Holding these in my mind, I offer them well
To the supreme beings, the Buddhas and
      Bodhisattvas.
O Compassionate Ones, holy objects of offering,
Think of me kindly and accept what I offer.

(7)   Lacking merit, I am destitute
And have nothing else that I can offer;
Therefore, O Protectors, who think of the welfare
      of others,
Please accept these for my sake.

(8)   Eternally I will offer all my bodies
To the Buddhas and Bodhisattvas.
Out of respect, I will become your servant;
Please accept me, O Supreme Heroes.

(9)   Being completely under your care,
I will benefit living beings with no fear of
      samsara.
I will purify my previous evils
And in future I will commit no more.

(10)   Within this sweetly scented bathing chamber
With a clear and glistening crystal floor,
Majestic pillars ablaze with jewels,
And canopies of radiant pearls spread aloft;

(11)   With many jewelled vases filled to the brim
With scented waters that steal the mind,
And to the accompaniment of music and song,
I offer ablution to the Buddhas and Bodhisattvas.

(12)   I dry their bodies with matchless cloths
That are immaculately clean and scented.
Then I offer to the holy beings
Fragrant garments in magnificent colours.

(13)   With various excellent raiments, fine and smooth,
And a multitude of supreme ornaments,
I adorn Arya Samantabhadra,
Manjushri, Avalokiteshvara and all the others.

(14)   Just like polishing pure, refined gold,
I anoint the radiant bodies of all the Able Ones
With supreme perfumes whose fragrance pervades
Every part of the three thousand worlds.

(15)   To the Able Ones, the supreme objects of offering,
I offer all the beautiful, scented flowers –
Mandaras, upalas, lotuses and so forth –
And exquisite garlands, finely arranged.

(16)   I offer them vast and fragrant clouds
Of supreme incense that steal the mind;
And I offer delicacies of the gods,
Together with a variety of food and drink.

(17)   I also offer jewelled lamps
       Arranged on golden lotuses;
       And on polished ground sprinkled with scent
       And scattered with beautiful flower petals,

(18)   I offer to those with the nature of compassion
       A celestial palace resounding with heavenly praise
       And hung with beautiful pearls and jewelled
            ornaments
       Whose infinite radiance illuminates space.

(19)   Eternally I will offer to the Able Ones
       Exquisite jewelled parasols held aloft,
       With pleasing shapes, handles of gold,
       And rims embellished with beautiful ornaments.

(20)   In addition to these, may masses of offerings
       Resounding with music and beautiful melodies
       Remain like so many clouds that send down relief
       To suffering living beings.

(21)   And upon all the holy Dharma Jewels,
       The stupas, and the images,
       May there fall an uninterrupted rain
       Of flowers, jewels and so forth.

(22)   Just as Manjushri, Samantabhadra, and others
       Made offerings to the Conquerors,
       So do I make offerings to the Sugatas,
            the Protectors,
       And to the Bodhisattvas.

(23)   To these oceans of good qualities,
I offer a melodious ocean of praise.
May a chorus of sweet-sounding melodious
    verses
Always ascend to their presence.

(24)   To all the Buddhas abiding in the three times,
The Dharma and the Supreme Assembly,
I prostrate with as many emanated bodies
As there are atoms in all the worlds.

(25)   I prostrate to the bases for generating bodhichitta,
To the images of Buddha's body, speech and
    mind,
To the Abbots and Preceptors,
And to the supreme practitioners on the path.

(26)   Until I attain the essence of great enlightenment,
I will go for refuge to the Buddhas;
Likewise, I will go for refuge to Dharma
And to the assembly of Bodhisattvas.

(27)   With my palms pressed together, I make requests
To those endowed with great compassion –
The perfect Buddhas and the Bodhisattvas,
Who abide throughout the ten directions.

(28)   Since beginningless time in samsara,
Throughout this and all my previous lives,
Out of ignorance I have committed evil,
Ordered it to be committed,

(29) And, overwhelmed by deceptive ignorance,
Rejoiced in its being committed by others.
Seeing all these to be grave mistakes,
From the depths of my heart I confess them to the
    holy beings.

(30) Whatever harmful actions of body, speech or mind
I have done under the influence of delusion
Towards the Three Precious Jewels,
My father and mother, my Spiritual Guide, and
    others –

(31) All the extremely unbearable evil actions
Committed by me, an evil person
Polluted by many faults –
I confess before the Deliverers, the enlightened
    beings.

(32) But I might die before I purify
All my negativities;
O Please protect me so that I
May surely and swiftly be freed from them.

(33) Since the untrustworthy Lord of Death
Will not wait while I purify my evils,
Regardless of whether I am sick or not,
This momentary life is unreliable.

(34) I shall have to leave everything and depart alone
But, through failing to understand this,
I have committed many kinds of evil action
With respect to my friends and others.

(35)   And yet my friends will become nothing
And others will also become nothing.
Even I shall become nothing;
Likewise, everything will become nothing.

(36)   Just like an experience in a dream,
Everything I now enjoy
Will become a mere recollection,
For what has passed cannot be seen again.

(37)   Even during this brief life,
Many friends and others have passed away;
But the unbearable results of the evil I have
    committed for their sake
Still lie ahead of me.

(38)   Thus, through failing to realize
That I shall suddenly die,
I have committed many evils
Out of ignorance, attachment and anger.

(39)   Remaining still neither day nor night,
This life is continuously slipping away
And never increases in duration;
So why should death not come to one
    such as me?

(40)   Even if, as I lie on my deathbed,
I am surrounded by friends and relatives,
I alone shall have to experience
The feeling of my life being severed.

(41)   Of what help will my companions be
When I am seized by the messengers of the Lord
     of Death?
At that time, only merit will protect me,
But upon that I have not relied.

(42)   O Protectors, oblivious to dangers such as these,
I, who am devoid of conscientiousness,
Have committed many negative actions
For the sake of this transient life.

(43)   Terrified is the person who today is led away
To a place where his limbs will be torn from
     his body.
With a dry mouth and sunken eyes,
His appearance is completely distorted.

(44)   So what need is there to mention the terrible
     despair
I shall experience when, stricken by great panic,
I am seized by the physical apparitions
Of the terrifying messengers of the Lord of Death?

(45)   'Who can grant me real protection
From this great terror?'
Petrified, with wide, bulging eyes,
I shall search for refuge in all directions,

(46)   But, seeing no refuge anywhere,
I shall become utterly dejected.
If I cannot find refuge there,
What shall I do at that time?

(47)   Therefore, from today I go for refuge
To the Conqueror Buddhas who protect living
    beings,
Who seek to give refuge to all living beings,
And who, with their great strength, eradicate
    all fear.

(48)   Likewise, I sincerely go for refuge
To the Dharma they have realized,
Which dispels the fears of samsara,
And to the assembly of Bodhisattvas.

(49)   Overcome with fear, I offer myself
To Arya Samantabhadra,
And I offer my body into the service
Of Arya Manjushri.

(50)   To Protector Avalokiteshvara,
Who acts unerringly out of compassion,
I utter this desperate cry for help:
'O Please protect me, an evildoer!'

(51)   Seeking refuge, from my heart
I pray to Arya Akashagarbha,
To Arya Ksitigarbha,
And to all the compassionate Protectors.

(52)   I go for refuge to Arya Vajrapani,
Upon sight of whom all harmful beings,
Such as the messengers of the Lord of Death,
Flee in terror to the four directions.

(53) Previously I transgressed your advice,
But now, having seen these great dangers,
I go to you for refuge
To quickly dispel my fears.

(54) If I need to follow the doctor's advice
When frightened by an ordinary illness,
How much more necessary is it to follow Buddha's
advice
When perpetually afflicted by the many harmful
diseases of the delusions?

(55) If all the people living in this world
Can be greatly harmed by just one of these
delusions,
And if no medicine other than Dharma
Can be found anywhere to cure them,

(56) Those who do not act in accordance with the
Dharma teachings
Given by Buddha, the all-knowing physician,
Through which all pains of the delusions can be
removed,
Are surely foolish and confused.

(57) If it is necessary to exercise caution
When near a small, ordinary precipice,
How much more necessary is it when near the
fathomless pits of hell
Into which I could fall for a very long time?

(58) It is unwise to indulge in pleasures,
Thinking, 'At least I shall not die today';
For without doubt the time will come
When I shall become nothing.

(59) Who will grant me fearlessness?
How can I be freed from these fears?
If I shall inevitably become nothing,
How can I continue to indulge?

(60) What remains with me now from the pleasant
experiences
Of my previous lives that have now ceased?
And yet, because of my strong attachment to
worldly pleasures,
I have gone against the advice of my Spiritual
Guide.

(61) If, when I depart from this life
And from my friends and relatives,
I must wander all alone,
Why commit non-virtue for the sake of friends and
enemies?

(62) 'How can I definitely be freed
From non-virtue, the source of all suffering?'
Throughout the day and the night,
I should think only about this.

(63) Whatever I have done
Out of unknowing and confusion –
Be it a natural non-virtue
Or a transgression –

(64)   With my palms pressed together
        And my mind fearful of suffering,
        Prostrating myself again and again,
        I confess them all before the Protectors.

(65)   I request all the holy beings
        To free me from all my evils and faults;
        And since these bring only harmful results,
        In future I will not commit them again.

This concludes the second chapter of *Guide to the Bodhisattva's Way of Life*, entitled 'Purifying Negativity'.

Chapter 3:

Generating Engaging Bodhichitta

Just as it is rare indeed
For a blind person to find a jewel in a heap of rubbish,
So too, by some very rare chance,
I have generated bodhichitta.

CHAPTER 3

Generating Engaging Bodhichitta

(1)   With great gladness I rejoice
       In the virtues that protect living beings
       From the sufferings of the lower realms
       And lead all those who suffer to fortunate realms.

(2)   I rejoice in the accumulation of virtue
       That releases living beings from samsaric rebirth
       And leads them to the state of nirvana –
       The supreme, permanent inner peace.

(3)   I rejoice in the enlightenment of the Conqueror
           Buddhas
       And in the spiritual paths of the Bodhisattvas.

(4)   With delight I rejoice in the ocean of virtue
       That arises from generating the mind of
           enlightenment, bodhichitta,
       Which brings happiness to all living beings,
       And in the deeds that benefit those beings.

(5)   To the Buddhas residing in all directions,
        With my palms pressed together I make this
            request:
        Please continue to shine the lamp of Dharma
        For living beings lost and suffering in the darkness
            of ignorance.

(6)   To the Conquerors who wish to enter parinirvana,
        With my palms pressed together I make this
            request:
        Please do not leave living beings in a state of
            blindness,
        But remain with us for countless aeons.

(7)   Thus, through the merit I have collected
        From all these virtuous actions,
        May the suffering of every living being
        Be brought completely to an end;

(8)   And until all those who are sick
        Have been cured of their illness,
        May I become their medicine,
        Their doctor and their nurse.

(9)   May a rain of food and drink descend
        To dispel the miseries of hunger and thirst;
        And during the great aeon of famine,
        May I become their food and drink.

(10)   May I become an inexhaustible treasury
        For the poor and destitute.
        May I be everything they might need,
        Placed freely at their disposal.

(11)   From this moment on, without any sense of loss,
       I shall give away my body and likewise my wealth,
       And my virtues amassed throughout the three times
       To help all living beings, my mothers.

(12)   Through giving all, I shall attain the nirvana of a
              Buddha
       And my bodhichitta wishes will be fulfilled.
       I give up everything for the sake of living beings,
       Who are the supreme objects of giving.

(13)   Since I have given up this body
       For the happiness of living beings,
       It will always be theirs to beat, to revile
       Or even to kill if they please.

(14)   Even if they play with it,
       Mock it or humiliate it,
       Since I have given this body to others,
       What is the point of holding it dear?

(15)   Therefore, in whatever I do,
       I will never cause harm to others;
       And whenever anyone encounters me,
       May it never be meaningless for them.

(16)   Whether those who encounter me
       Generate faith or anger,
       May it always be the cause
       Of their fulfilling all their wishes.

(17)   May all those who harm me –
       Whether verbally or by other means –
       And those who otherwise insult me
       Thereby create the cause to attain enlightenment.

(18) May I become a protector for the protectorless,
A guide for those who travel on the road,
And, for those who wish to cross the water,
May I become a boat, a ship or a bridge.

(19) May I become an island for those seeking dry land,
A lamp for those needing light,
A place of rest for those who desire one,
And a servant for those needing service.

(20) To benefit all living beings,
May I become a treasury of wealth,
Powerful mantras, potent medicine,
A wish-fulfilling tree and a wish-granting cow.

(21) Just like the great elements such as earth,
And like eternal space,
May I become the basis from which everything arises
For sustaining the life of countless living beings;

(22) And, until they have passed beyond sorrow,
May I sustain all forms of life
Throughout the realms of living beings
That reach to the ends of space.

(23) Just as all the previous Sugatas, the Buddhas,
Generated the mind of enlightenment, bodhichitta,
And accomplished all the stages
Of the Bodhisattva's training,

(24) So will I too, for the sake of all beings,
Generate the mind of enlightenment
And accomplish all the stages
Of the Bodhisattva's training.

(25)   The wise who have sincerely taken up
       The mind of enlightenment in this way,
       So as to maintain it and increase it
       Should encourage themselves as follows.

(26)   Now my life has borne great fruit,
       My human life has attained great meaning;
       Today I am born into the lineage of Buddha
       And have become a Bodhisattva.

(27)   All my actions from now on
       Shall accord with this noble lineage;
       And upon this lineage, pure and faultless,
       I shall never bring disgrace.

(28)   Just as it is rare indeed
       For a blind person to find a jewel in a heap of
           rubbish,
       So too, by some very rare chance,
       I have generated bodhichitta.

(29)   It is the supreme nectar that overcomes
       The dominion of death over living beings,
       And an inexhaustible treasury
       That dispels all their poverty.

(30)   It is the supreme medicine that relieves
       The sickness of living beings,
       And a shady tree that provides shelter
       For weary beings travelling samsara's paths.

(31)   It is a universal bridge by which all living beings
       Can be delivered from the lower realms,
       And a rising moon of a mind
       That relieves the torment of their delusions.

(32)   It is a vast sun that completely dispels
       The fog of unknowing from living beings.
       It is the quintessential butter that arises
       When the milk of Dharma is churned.

(33)   For the honoured guests, the beings on samsara's
            paths
       Who wish to enjoy the delights of bliss,
       Bodhichitta will satisfy them all
       By leading them to the supreme state of bliss.

(34)   Today, in the presence of all the Protectors,
       I invite all living beings to be my guests
       To enjoy these temporary and ultimate delights.
       May gods, demi-gods and everyone else be joyful!

This concludes the third chapter of *Guide to the Bodhisattva's Way of Life*, entitled 'Generating Engaging Bodhichitta'.

Chapter 4:

Relying upon Conscientiousness

It is for these reasons that Buddha, the Blessed One, said
That it is extremely difficult to obtain a precious
    human life;
Just as it is rare for a turtle to insert its neck
Into a yoke adrift on a vast ocean.

CHAPTER 4

Relying upon Conscientiousness

(1)   A practitioner who has firmly generated
      Aspiring and engaging bodhichitta in this way
      Should always apply effort without wavering
      So as not to stray from the trainings.

(2)   If an ordinary action is undertaken in haste
      Or without being well thought out,
      It might be appropriate to reconsider,
      Even if a promise has been made;

(3)   But how could I possibly turn back
      From something that has been examined
      By the wisdom of the Buddhas and Bodhisattvas,
      And that I too have repeatedly examined?

(4)   If, having made the bodhichitta promise,
        I do not actually put it into practice,
        Since I shall be deceiving all these living beings,
        What sort of rebirth shall I then take?

(5)   It is said that someone who, out of miserliness,
        Does not give even the smallest ordinary thing
        That he or she has dedicated to others
        Will be reborn as a hungry spirit.

(6)   So, if I were to deceive all living beings,
        Whom from the depths of my heart I have invited
        To be guests at the banquet of enlightenment,
        How could I take a fortunate rebirth in the future?

(7)   How someone who abandons bodhichitta
        Can then attain liberation
        Is beyond ordinary comprehension –
        Only the omniscient can know that.

(8)   For a Bodhisattva, abandoning bodhichitta
        Is the heaviest of all downfalls
        For, should he or she incur it,
        The whole basis of working for others will be lost.

(9)   And if someone else were to obstruct or hinder
        A Bodhisattva's virtuous actions, even for a
            moment,
        Since he would be undermining the welfare of all
            living beings,
        There would be no end to his lower rebirths.

(10) For if I would experience misfortune
As a result of destroying the happiness of just one
    being,
What can be said of the consequences of destroying
The happiness of all living beings as extensive as
    space?

(11) Those who repeatedly renew their Bodhisattva vow
Only to go on to incur further downfalls
Will remain for a long time enmeshed in samsara,
Obstructed from attaining higher spiritual grounds.

(12) Therefore, I must practise sincerely,
In accordance with the promise I have made.
If, from now on, I make no effort,
I shall be reborn in lower and lower states.

(13) Even though there have been countless Buddhas in
    the past
Working to benefit all living beings,
Because I have so many karmic obstacles
I have not been a direct object of their care;

(14) And, if I remain like this,
Again and again I shall have to experience
Sickness, incarceration, laceration,
And mutilation in the lower realms.

(15) Since the appearance of a Tathagata – a Buddha,
Faith in his teachings, a precious human body,
And a suitable basis for practising Dharma are so
    rare,
When will an opportunity like this arise again?

(16)   Today, for example, I might be free from sickness,
       Well-nourished and without afflictions;
       But this life is fleeting and deceptive,
       And my body is as if borrowed for a moment.

(17)   If I engage in non-virtuous actions,
       I shall not obtain a human body again;
       And if I do not attain a human form,
       There will be no virtue, only negativity.

(18)   If I do not practise virtue now
       While I have the good fortune to do so,
       What virtue shall I be able to practise
       When I am suffering and confused in the lower
            realms?

(19)   For if I do not practise virtue
       But accumulate only evil,
       I shall not even hear the words 'fortunate rebirth'
       For a hundred million aeons.

(20)   It is for these reasons that Buddha, the Blessed One,
            said
       That it is extremely difficult to obtain a precious
            human life;
       Just as it is rare for a turtle to insert its neck
       Into a yoke adrift on a vast ocean.

(21)   Since just one moment of evil
       Can lead to an aeon in the deepest hell,
       If I do not purify all the evil I have collected since
            beginningless time,
       It goes without saying that I shall not take a human
            rebirth.

(22)   Simply experiencing the effects of my non-virtue
       Will not lead to my being released from the lower
           realms,
       For, while I am experiencing those effects,
       I shall be generating yet more non-virtue.

(23)   If, having found the freedom and endowment of
           a human life,
       I do not strive to practise Dharma,
       There can be no greater self-deception,
       There can be no greater folly.

(24)   Having understood this,
       If out of ignorance I remain indolent,
       Then, when the time comes for me to die,
       I shall be choked with unimaginable terror.

(25)   If my body will burn for a very long time
       In the unbearable fires of hell,
       Then, without doubt, my mind will be consumed
       By the raging fires of regret.

(26)   Having found, by some very slight chance,
       This beneficial state, so rare to find,
       If, while I am endowed with such good fortune,
       I am once again led to the hells,

(27)   It is as if I am confused by a spell
       And my mind has been reduced to nothing!
       Even I do not know what causes this confusion –
       What is it that dwells within me?

(28)   The inner enemies of hatred, attachment and
            so forth
        Do not have arms and legs,
        Nor do they have courage or skill;
        So how have they made me their slave?

(29)   While they remain within my mind,
        They harm me at their pleasure,
        And yet, without anger, I patiently endure them.
        How shameful! This is no occasion for patience.

(30)   If all living beings, including the gods and
            demi-gods,
        Were to rise up against me as one enemy,
        They could not lead me to the fires of the deepest
            hell
        And throw me in;

(31)   But this powerful enemy of the delusions
        In an instant can cast me into that fiery place
        Where even the ashes of Mount Meru
        Would be consumed without a trace.

(32)   No other type of enemy
        Can remain for as long a time
        As can the enduring foes of my delusions,
        For they have no beginning and no apparent end.

(33)   If I agree with external enemies and honour them,
        They will eventually bring me benefit and
            happiness;
        But if I entrust myself to delusions,
        In the future they will bring me only more pain
            and suffering.

(34)   So how can I remain in samsara joyfully and
            without fear
        While I readily reserve a place in my heart
        For this interminable enemy of long duration
        That alone is the cause of increasing all my suffering?

(35)   How can I ever be happy
        While these guardians of the prison of samsara
        That torture and torment me in the hells and
            elsewhere
        Dwell like a net of iron in my mind?

(36)   Out of anger, worldly people who are filled with
            pride will not sleep
        Until they have destroyed those who cause them
            even the slightest temporary harm.
        In the same way, I will not abandon my efforts
        Until this inner foe of mine is directly and definitely
            destroyed.

(37)   If those who engage in violent battles,
        Strongly wishing to destroy deluded beings who
            must suffer death anyway,
        Disregard the pain of being wounded by weapons
        And do not withdraw until they have accomplished
            their aim,

(38)   Then it goes without saying that, even if I have to
            endure great hardships,
        From now on I should not be indolent or
            faint-hearted
        In striving once and for all to destroy this natural foe
        That is the constant source of all my suffering.

(39) If scars inflicted by enemies for no great reason
      Are displayed on the body like ornaments,
      Why should I not be prepared to endure hardships
      In striving sincerely to accomplish the great
          purpose?

(40) If fishermen, hunters and farmers,
      Who think only of their own livelihood,
      Endure such sufferings as heat and cold,
      Why can I not forbear hardships for the sake of the
          happiness of all?

(41) If I myself am not free from delusions
      When I promise all living beings
      Abiding in the ten directions throughout space
      That I will liberate them from *their* delusions,

(42) Is it not foolish of me to say such things
      While disregarding my own shortcomings?
      This being so, I must never turn back
      From destroying my own delusions.

(43) This will be my main objective:
      Bearing a strong grudge, to do battle with my
          delusions.
      Although such a grudge appears to be a delusion,
      Because it destroys delusions it is not.

(44) It would be better for me to be burned to death
      Or to have my head cut off
      Than to ever allow myself
      To come under the influence of delusions.

(45)   An ordinary enemy who is expelled from a country
Will go to another and remain there,
Only to return when he has regained his strength;
But the enemy of the delusions is not like that.

(46)   O delusions, delusions, where will you go
When banished by the eye of wisdom and expelled
    from my mind?
And from where will you return to harm me again?
But, being weak-minded, I am reduced to making no
    effort!

(47)   The delusions are not in the objects, in the sense
    powers, between them, or elsewhere;
So from where can they cause harm to all living
    beings?
Because they are just like illusions, I should banish
    fear from my heart and strive to attain wisdom.
Why bring the sufferings of hell and so forth upon
    myself for no reason?

(48)   Therefore, having considered this well,
I will strive sincerely to practise these precepts as
    they have been explained.
If a sick person does not listen to the doctor's advice,
How can he expect to be cured?

This concludes the fourth chapter of *Guide to the Bodhisattva's Way of Life*, entitled 'Relying upon Conscientiousness'.

Chapter 5:

Guarding the Mind

with Alertness

A crazy, untamed elephant in this world
Cannot inflict such harm
As the sufferings of the deepest hell
Caused by the rampaging elephant of the mind;

CHAPTER 5

Guarding the Mind
with Alertness

(1) Those who wish to make progress in the trainings
Should be very attentive in guarding their minds,
For, if they do not practise guarding the mind,
They will not be able to complete the trainings.

(2) A crazy, untamed elephant in this world
Cannot inflict such harm
As the sufferings of the deepest hell
Caused by the rampaging elephant of the mind;

(3) But if the elephant of our mind
Is bound tightly on all sides by the rope of
    mindfulness,
All fears will cease to exist
And all virtues will fall into our hands.

(4)   Tigers, lions, elephants, bears,
       Snakes, all kinds of enemy,
       Guardians of the beings in hell,
       Evil spirits and cannibals –

(5)   These will all be bound
       Simply by binding the mind,
       And will all be subdued
       Simply by subduing the mind.

(6)   Buddha, the Able One, says,
       'Thus, all fears
       And all infinite sufferings
       Arise from the mind.'

(7)   Who purposely creates the weapons
       That harm the beings in the hells?
       Who creates the blazing iron ground?
       From where do the tempting hallucinations arise?

(8)   The Able One says that all such things
       Come only from evil minds.
       Thus, there is nothing to fear within the three worlds
       That has not come from the mind.

(9)   If completing the perfection of giving
       Were eliminating the poverty of living beings,
       Since hungry beings still exist,
       How could the previous Buddhas have completed
           that perfection?

(10)   The completion of the perfection of giving is said
           to be
       The thought wishing to give everything to all
           living beings,

Together with the merit that results from that giving;
Therefore, it depends only on mind.

(11)   The killing of fish and other creatures
Has not been eradicated anywhere,
For completing the perfection of moral discipline is
    said to be
Attaining a mind that has abandoned non-virtue.

(12)   It is not possible to subdue unruly beings
Who are as extensive as space;
But simply destroying the mind of anger
Is the same as overcoming all these foes.

(13)   Where is there enough leather
To cover the surface of the Earth?
But just having leather on the soles of one's feet
Is the same as covering the whole Earth.

(14)   In the same way, it is not possible
To control all external events;
But, if I simply control my mind,
What need is there to control other things?

(15)   Rebirth as a first form realm god and so on, the
    highest level of mundane happiness,
Which results from the mental action of clear
    concentration of the actual absorption* of the form
    or formless realms,
Does not come from actions of body or speech
But from actions of mind.

* The two absorptions – the absorption of close preparation
and the actual absorption – can be understood from the book
Ocean of Nectar.

(16)   Buddha, the All Knowing One, has said
       That reciting mantras and prayers, and enduring
           spiritual hardships,
       Even for a long time,
       Are to no avail if the mind is distracted elsewhere.

(17)   Even those who wish to find happiness and avoid
           suffering
       Will wander without meaning or purpose
       If they do not practise training the mind,
       The supreme and principal Dharma.

(18)   Therefore, I will guard my mind well
       And protect it from what is inappropriate.
       Without the discipline of guarding the mind,
       What is the use of many other disciplines?

(19)   Just as I would be careful of a wound
       When in a jostling and unruly crowd,
       So should I always guard the wound of my mind
       When among those who might provoke delusions.

(20)   If I am careful of a physical wound
       Out of fear of even the slightest pain,
       Why do I not protect the wound of my mind
       Out of fear of being crushed by the mountains of
           hell?

(21)   If I always practise in this way,
       Then, whether I am among harmful beings
       Or with people I find attractive,
       Neither my steadfastness nor my vows will
           decline.

(22) I can accept losing my wealth and reputation,
Or even my livelihood or my body,
And I can even accept my other virtues
     degenerating;
But I can never allow my practice of guarding the
     mind to decline.

(23) With my palms pressed together,
I beseech those who wish to guard their minds:
Always put effort into guarding
Both mindfulness and alertness.

(24) Just as people who are troubled by sickness
Have no strength for any kind of physical work,
So those whose minds are disturbed by confusion
Have no strength for any kind of virtuous action.

(25) Moreover, for those whose minds lack alertness,
The wisdoms from listening, contemplating and
     meditating
Will not be retained by their memory
Any more than water will remain in a leaky pot.

(26) Even those who have much learning and faith
And who have sincerely applied great effort
Will become defiled by moral downfalls
Through the fault of lacking alertness.

(27) If I lack alertness, the thieves of the delusions
Will cause my mindfulness to degenerate,
And then steal even the merit I have so diligently
     gathered
So that I shall fall into the lower realms.

(28) These legions of thieves of the delusions
Are just waiting for an opportunity
And, when one arises, they will steal my wealth of
virtue
And destroy any chance of a fortunate rebirth.

(29) Therefore, I will not allow my mindfulness
To stray from the doorway of my mind;
And, if I notice it is about to leave,
I will restore it by recalling the sufferings of the
lower realms.

(30) Fortunate ones who follow the instructions they
receive,
Maintain respect for their Spiritual Guide
And generate fear of the lower realms
Can easily develop and maintain mindfulness.

(31) 'I am always in the presence
Of the Buddhas and Bodhisattvas
Who, with their omniscient gaze,
See everything without obstruction.'

(32) By thinking in this way, we can maintain
Sense of shame, respect and fear,
And repeatedly bring to mind
The good qualities of the Buddhas.

(33) When mindfulness is maintained
With the purpose of guarding the mind,
Alertness will naturally arise
And even that which was lost will return.

(34) First, I should check to see how my mind is;
      And, if I see it is polluted with negativity,
      I should remain unmoving,
      With a mind as impassive as wood.

(35) I should never look around
      Out of distraction or for no purpose,
      But always, with a resolute mind,
      Be mindful of my gaze.

(36) From time to time, to relax my gaze,
      I should look around without distraction;
      And if someone appears in my field of vision,
      I should acknowledge them and greet them.

(37) To avoid dangers or accidents on the path,
      I should occasionally look in all directions,
      And prevent my mind from becoming distracted
      By relying upon conscientiousness.

(38) I should practise in the same way
      Whenever I go or return.
      Understanding the need to behave like this,
      I should apply this practice in all situations.

(39) I should prepare for any activity by thinking,
      'My body and mind must remain correctly
          composed';
      And from time to time check carefully to see
      What I am actually doing and thinking.

(40) With all my effort, I should regularly check
      That the unsubdued elephant of my mind
      Has not broken free but remains bound
      To the great pillar of thinking about Dharma.

(41)   Striving for concentration by whatever means,
I should not let my mind wander for even a moment
But closely examine it by asking,
'How is my mind behaving?'

(42)   It is said there are times, when practising giving,
that one can be judicious
In applying some of the finer points of moral
discipline.
When there is danger or a special celebration,
One can perform actions suitable for that occasion.

(43)   I should undertake what I intend and have decided
to do,
Without being distracted by other things;
And, with my thoughts focused on that practice,
For now, I should do just that.

(44)   In this way, I shall do everything well;
Otherwise, I shall accomplish neither one thing nor
the other.
With this skilful practice, there can be no increase
In secondary delusions, such as non-alertness.

(45)   Whenever I listen to any sort of talk,
Whether pleasant or unpleasant,
Or observe attractive or unattractive people,
I should prevent attachment or hatred towards them.

(46)   If for no reason I begin to perform actions
That cause damage to the environment,
I should recall Buddha's advice
And, out of respect, stop straightaway.

(47)   Whenever I wish to move my body
       Or to utter any words,
       I should first examine my mind
       And then steadfastly act in an appropriate way.

(48)   Whenever there arises in my mind
       The desire to become attached or angry,
       I should not do or say anything
       But remain as impassive as wood.

(49)   Whenever I am pretentious, mocking,
       Arrogant or self-important;
       Whenever I develop the intention to speak of
            others' faults,
       Or think of profiteering or deceiving;

(50)   Or whenever I start to solicit praise,
       Deprecate others,
       Or use harmful or divisive speech,
       I should remain as impassive as wood.

(51)   Whenever I desire wealth, honour or fame,
       Or the attentions of a circle of admirers;
       Or whenever my mind wishes for veneration,
       I should remain as impassive as wood.

(52)   If I develop a mind wishing to say something,
       While neglecting others' welfare
       And pursuing only my own,
       I should remain as impassive as wood.

(53) If I am ever impatient with suffering, or lazy and
         fearful of virtue;
      If I am about to speak recklessly or disparagingly;
      Or if attachment to my circle of acquaintances arises,
      I should remain as impassive as wood.

(54) Thus, having checked thoroughly for delusions
      And minds that are drawn to meaningless things,
      Courageous practitioners should hold their mind
         steady
      Through applying the appropriate opponents.

(55) With complete certainty, strong faith,
      Steadfastness, respect, politeness,
      Sense of shame, fearfulness, and inner peace,
      I should strive to bring joy to others.

(56) I should not become disheartened by the behaviour
         of others –
      The childish, who are in disharmony with one
         another –
      But understand how this behaviour arises through
         the force of delusions
      And be compassionate towards them.

(57) I should engage only in virtuous actions
      To benefit living beings, with no thought for myself;
      And I should do so with the understanding that I
         am like an illusion
      That does not exist from its own side.

(58)   Contemplating again and again
       That I have attained this special freedom after a
            very long time,
       I should hold as unmoveable as Mount Meru
       The intention to accomplish the real meaning of a
            human life.

(59)   If, mind, you are concerned
       About death taking this body from you
       And its being burned or buried beneath the ground,
       Why do you cherish it so now?

(60)   Why, mind, do you hold this body as 'mine'
       And grasp it with such affection?
       It is only borrowed from others
       And will soon be taken from you.

(61)   Why, confused mind,
       Do you not hold onto a clean wooden form?
       What is the use of grasping at this putrid machine
       That is only a collection of impurities?

(62)   Begin by mentally separating
       The layers of skin from the flesh.
       Then, with the blade of wisdom,
       Cut the flesh away from the bones.

(63)   Break open even the bones
       And look right down to the marrow.
       Make your own investigation –
       'Where is its essence?'

(64)   If you do not find any essence there
       Even when you search with such effort,
       Why, mind, do you still grasp this body
       With so much attachment?

(65)   It is so impure, it is not even fit to eat,
       Its blood is not fit to drink
       And its intestines are not fit to suck;
       So what use is this body to you?

(66)   It is suitable to protect it and care for it
       Only for attaining spiritual goals –
       This body of a human being
       Should be used just for practising Dharma.

(67)   But if you guard it for other purposes,
       What will you be able to do
       When the merciless Lord of Death seizes it
       And reduces it to a pile of ashes?

(68)   A servant is not rewarded with clothes and the like
       If he does no work;
       So why do you insist on nourishing this collection
           of flesh and bone
       When, even when fed, its loyalties lie elsewhere?

(69)   In exchange for paying my body its wages,
       I will employ it to create virtue for myself and
           others;
       But I should not grasp it as 'mine'
       Because such grasping is a form of ignorance.

(70)   I will regard my body as a boat –
       A basis for coming and going –
       And to accomplish the welfare of all living beings
       I will transform my body into an enlightened
           wishfulfilling jewel.

(71)   While I have control,
       I should always display a smiling face
       And, forsaking frowns and angry looks,
       Be friendly and honest towards others.

(72)   I should not behave in ways that disturb others,
       Such as moving furniture noisily
       Or opening and closing doors loudly,
       But always delight in humility.

(73)   Just as a stork, a cat or a thief
       Accomplish their aims with skill and patience,
       So should I accomplish my spiritual goal
       Of attaining the state of enlightenment.

(74)   When others offer wise advice or admonishment
       That, though unsolicited, is nevertheless beneficial,
       I should accept it graciously and with respect,
       And always be willing to learn from it.

(75)   To anyone who speaks the truth,
       I should say, 'You have spoken well';
       And whenever I see others perform meritorious
           actions,
       I should offer praise and develop genuine joy.

(76)   I should discreetly describe others' good qualities
       And pass on any I hear about,
       But, should my own good qualities be mentioned,
       I should simply acknowledge any I might have,
           without pride.

(77)   I should perform all actions for others' happiness.
       This good quality is precious and rare,
       And through it I shall enjoy the pure happiness
           and joy
       That arises from actions that benefit others.

(78)   If I do this, I shall suffer no loss in this life
       And in future lives I shall experience great
           happiness;
       But, if I do the opposite,
       I shall experience misery and pain in life after life.

(79)   I should speak truthfully, coherently and to the
           point,
       Making my meaning clear in a pleasant manner.
       I should speak gently and in moderation,
       Without a selfish motivation.

(80)   Whenever I see other beings,
       I should think, 'I can attain enlightenment
       In dependence upon these living beings!'
       And cherish them sincerely.

(81)   With either a cultivated motivation
       Or one that arises spontaneously,
       I should always sow seeds of great virtue
       In the fields of holy beings and living beings.

(82)   I should perform all my Dharma activities
       With skill, clear understanding and strong faith,
       So that others will increase their wisdom
       And experience immeasurable benefit.

(83)   Although in general the perfections of giving and
          so forth
       Are progressively higher than those that precede
          them,
       I should not forsake great virtues for the sake of
          small ones.
       Principally, I should consider the benefit to others.

(84)   Buddha, the compassionate Far-Seeing One,
       Allows Bodhisattvas to perform certain actions that
          are otherwise proscribed.
       Understanding this well, I should always put effort
       Into my practice of the Bodhisattva's way of life.

(85)   I should share my food with animals,
       People who are hungry and practitioners,
       And eat merely what I need.
       Ordained people can give everything except their
          three robes.

(86)   Because I use this body to practise bodhichitta,
       I should not harm it for the sake of temporary
          benefits,
       But care for it so that I may fulfil my bodhichitta
          wish,
       So that eventually all living beings' wishes will be
          fulfilled.

(87) Those who lack pure compassion and wisdom
Should not actually give away their body
But, instead, devote it to accomplishing
The great purpose of this and future lives.

(88) I should listen to Dharma
With respect and a good heart,
Recognizing it as the supreme medicine
For curing the pains of anger and attachment.

(89) I should teach the vast and profound Dharma with
a pure intention,
Free from any wish to acquire wealth or reputation;
And I should always maintain a pure motivation of
bodhichitta
And make great effort to put Dharma into practice.

(90) I should explain Dharma to release those who are
listening
From samsara, the cycle of suffering,
And to lead them to the ultimate goal –
The attainment of full enlightenment.

(91) I should keep places clean and not throw litter
But dispose of it correctly.
Moreover, I should not defile
Water or land used by others.

(92) I should not eat with my mouth full,
Noisily or with my mouth open.
I should not sit with my legs outstretched,
Nor rub my hands together meaninglessly.

(93) I should not sit alone with another's partner
In a vehicle, on a bed or in the same room.
I should observe and enquire about what offends
     people
And then avoid such actions.

(94) To show someone the way,
I should not point with just one finger
But respectfully use my right hand
With all the fingers extended.

(95) I should not wave my arms around in an
          uncontrolled manner,
But communicate with slight movements
And appropriate gestures;
Otherwise, I shall lose my composure.

(96) To sleep, I should lie in the appropriate position –
Just as Protector Buddha lay when he entered
          parinirvana –
And before falling asleep, with alertness,
Make a definite decision to rise quickly.

(97) Within the limitless practices
Taught as the Bodhisattva's way of life,
I should start by emphasizing
These practices that train the mind.

(98) I should practise the *Sutra of the Three Heaps*
Three times each day and three times each night,
And, with reliance on the Three Jewels and
          bodhichitta,
Purify non-virtues and downfalls.

(99)   Whatever I do in any situation,
       Whether for myself or for the benefit of others,
       I should strive to practise
       Whatever training has been taught for that occasion.

(100) For a Bodhisattva, there is no teaching of Buddha
       That he or she should not practise.
       If I become skilled in this way of life,
       Nothing I do will lack merit.

(101) Whether directly or indirectly,
       I should never do anything that is not for the sake
            of living beings.
       I should dedicate everything
       Solely to the enlightenment of all living beings.

(102) Never, even at the cost of my life,
       Should I abandon my Spiritual Guide,
       Who is skilled in the meaning of the Mahayana
       And a supreme practitioner of the Bodhisattva
            trainings.

(103) I should train in relying upon the Spiritual Guide
       In the manner explained in the *Biography of Shri
            Sambhava*.
       I can understand this and other advice given by
            Buddha
       From studying the Mahayana Sutras.

(104) I should read these Sutras
       Because they reveal the Bodhisattva trainings.
       First, it is important to study
       Akashagarbha Sutra.

(105) Also, it is important to read again and again
The *Compendium of Trainings*
Because it extensively reveals
What is to be practised all the time.

(106) Moreover, sometimes one should read
The *Condensed Compendium of Sutras*;
And with great effort, one should also study
The same two titles by Superior Nagarjuna.

(107) In summary, since I generated engaging bodhichitta
and took the Bodhisattva vow,
I should practise all the precepts mentioned
above,
So that others' pure view, mind of faith and good
intention
Will be increased by my example.

(108) The defining characteristic of guarding alertness
Is to examine again and again
The state of our body, speech and mind,
And to understand whether our actions are correct
or not.

(109) We need to put Buddha's teachings, the Dharma,
into practice
Because nothing can be accomplished just by
reading words.
A sick man will never be cured of his illness
Through merely reading medical instructions!

This concludes the fifth chapter of *Guide to the Bodhisattva's Way of Life*, entitled 'Guarding the Mind with Alertness'.

Chapter 6:

Relying upon Patience

If, for example, a house caught fire
And there was a danger of the fire spreading to an
adjacent house,
It would be advisable to remove anything, such as
dry grass,
That might enable the fire to spread.

CHAPTER 6

Relying upon Patience

(1) All the virtuous deeds and merit,
     Such as giving and making offerings,
     That we have accumulated over thousands of aeons
     Can be destroyed by just one moment of anger.

(2) There is no evil greater than anger,
     And no virtue greater than patience.
     Therefore, I should strive in various ways
     To become familiar with the practice of patience.

(3) If I harbour painful thoughts of anger,
     I shall not experience mental peace,
     I shall find no joy or happiness,
     And I shall be unsettled and unable to sleep.

(4) Overcome by a fit of anger,
     I might even kill a benefactor
     Upon whose kindness I depend
     For my wealth or reputation.

(5) Anger causes friends and relatives to grow weary
of me
And, even if I try to attract them with generosity,
they will not trust me.
In short, there is no one
Who can live happily with anger.

(6) Although the enemy of anger
Creates sufferings such as these,
Whoever works hard to overcome it
Will find only happiness in this and future lives.

(7) Through having to do what I do not want to do
Or being prevented from doing what I want to do,
I develop mental unhappiness, which becomes
the fuel
That causes anger to grow and destroy me.

(8) Therefore, I should never allow this fuel of mental
unhappiness
That causes anger to grow within my mind,
For this enemy of anger has no function
Other than to harm me.

(9) I will not allow anything that happens to me
To disturb my mental peace.
If I become unhappy, I shall be unable to fulfil my
spiritual wishes
And my practice of virtue will decline.

(10) If something can be remedied
Why be unhappy about it?
And if there is no remedy for it,
There is still no point in being unhappy.

(11) People do not want suffering, criticism,
Harsh words or anything unpleasant
For themselves or for their friends;
But for their enemies it is the opposite!

(12) In samsara, the causes of happiness rarely occur,
Whereas the causes of suffering are innumerable.
Without suffering, there would be no renunciation;
Therefore, mind, you should remain firm.

(13) If some ascetics and the people of Karnapa
Can endure the pain of burns and cuts for no great
purpose,
Why can I not endure hardships
For the sake of liberating everyone from their
suffering?

(14) There is nothing that is not easy to accomplish
If we develop familiarity with it;
So first I should learn to forbear small sufferings
And then gradually endure greater ones.

(15) This can be seen in those who voluntarily endure
minor sufferings,
Such as animal or insect bites,
Feelings of hunger or thirst,
Or irritations of the skin.

(16) I should not become impatient
With heat and cold, wind and rain,
Or sickness, confinement or beatings;
For, if I do, the pain will only increase.

(17)   Some, when they see their own blood,
       Become even stronger and braver;
       While for others, just seeing someone else's blood
       Causes them to become weak and even to faint!

(18)   Both these reactions depend on the mind –
       Whether it is strong or it is weak –
       So I should disregard any harm that befalls me
       And not allow myself to be affected by suffering.

(19)   Whenever I experience hardship,
       I should fight my delusions, such as anger;
       And whenever I experience physical pain,
       I should use wisdom to maintain a pure and
           peaceful mind.

(20)   Those who disregard all suffering
       To destroy the foes of anger and so forth
       Are the true conquerors worthy of the name 'hero';
       Other so-called heroes merely slay corpses.

(21)   Moreover, suffering has many good qualities.
       Through experiencing it, we can dispel pride,
       Develop compassion for those trapped in samsara,
       Abandon non-virtue and delight in virtue.

(22)   I do not become angry when the cause of suffering
       Is something inanimate, such as sickness;
       So why become angry with animate causes,
       For they too are all controlled by other conditions?

(23)   Although it is not wished for in the least,
       Sickness nevertheless occurs.
       In the same way, even though they are not wanted,
       Delusions such as anger forcibly arise.

(24)   People do not think, 'I will get angry',
They just get angry;
And anger does not think, 'I will arise',
It just arises.

(25)   All the shortcomings there are,
And all the various non-virtues,
Arise through the force of other conditions –
They do not govern themselves.

(26)   The assembled conditions have no thought
To produce a suffering result;
Nor does the resultant suffering think,
'I was produced from conditions.'

(27)   Neither that which is asserted as the 'independent
creator of all'
Nor that which is asserted as the 'independent
permanent self'
Can come into being through intentionally thinking,
'Now I will arise.'

(28)   If the independent creator itself is not produced,
Then how can it produce anything?
If the self were permanent, then it would follow
That experiences cannot be changed from
unpleasant to pleasant.

(29)   Clearly, if the self were permanent,
Then, just like space, it could not perform any
actions;
And, even if it could meet with other conditions,
It would still be unable to do anything.

(30)   Since, even when acted upon, it would remain as
            it was,
        What effect could an action have on it?
        If you say that something else affects the self,
        What relationship could the self have with that?

(31)   Thus, all effects arise from other conditions,
        Which in turn depend upon previous conditions.
        Therefore, all things are like illusions – they are not
            independent.
        If we realize this, we shall not become angry with
            anything.

(32)   *'If all things were like illusions, who would restrain what?*
        Surely, any restraint would be inappropriate.'
        On the contrary, it is precisely because things lack
            inherent existence
        That it is possible to assert that the continuum of
            suffering can be cut.

(33)   Thus, whenever an enemy, or even a friend,
        Commits an inappropriate action,
        Such behaviour arises from other conditions.
        Realizing this, I should remain with a happy mind.

(34)   If things occurred independently, out of choice,
        Then, since no one wishes to suffer,
        How would suffering ever arise
        For any living being?

(35)   Some misguided people inflict harm upon
            themselves
        By lying on thorns and the like;
        While others, obsessed with finding a partner,
        Deprive themselves of food.

(36)   Then there are those who inflict harm on
            themselves
        Through non-meritorious actions,
        Such as hanging themselves, leaping from cliffs,
        Swallowing poison or eating bad food.

(37)   Although they cherish themselves more than
            anything else,
        If, under the influence of delusions, people are
            capable even of killing themselves,
        Why should I be surprised when they inflict harm
        On other living beings such as me?

(38)   When those who, under the influence of delusions,
        Set out to harm or even to kill me,
        If I cannot develop compassion for them,
        At the very least I should refrain from getting
            angry.

(39)   If it were the very nature of a childish person
        To inflict harm on others,
        It would be no more reasonable to get angry with
            him
        Than it would be to resent fire for burning us.

(40)   On the other hand, if that harmfulness were a
           temporary fault
       And that person were otherwise good-natured,
       It would be just as unreasonable to get angry with
           him
       As it would be to resent space for filling with smoke.

(41)   If someone were to harm us with a stick or other
           weapon,
       We would normally become angry with the person;
       But, since his intent is governed by anger,
       It is really towards that anger that we should direct
           our wrath.

(42)   In such situations, we should think,
       'In the past, I harmed others in a similar manner.
       Therefore, it is fitting that I, who caused harm to
           others,
       Should now be experiencing such harm myself.'

(43)   The physical suffering I experience
       Is caused by both the stick and my body;
       But, since the stick comes from my assailant and
           the body from me,
       With which of these should I get angry?

(44)   Blinded by craving and ignorance,
       I have taken this form, the basis of human suffering,
       Which can hardly bear to be touched;
       So with whom should I get angry when it is hurt?

(45)   Although we childish beings have no wish for
        suffering,
    We are greatly attached to its causes.
    Thus, the harm we receive is entirely our fault;
    What reason is there to blame it on others?

(46)   Just as with the guardians of hell,
    The forest of razor-sharp leaves and so forth,
    My sufferings in this life result from my actions –
    So with whom should I be angry?

(47)   Although those who harm me
    Are provoked into doing so by my own karma,
    It is *they* who will take rebirth in hell as a result;
    So, is it not I who harm them?

(48)   By depending upon them as my objects of patience,
    I can purify many non-virtues;
    But by depending upon me as their object of anger,
    They will fall for a long time into hellish states of
        suffering.

(49)   Thus, since it is I who inflict harm on them
    And they who benefit me,
    Why, unruly mind, do you distort things so
    By becoming angry with them?

(50)   If I maintain this positive view,
    I shall not create the cause to be reborn in hell;
    But, although I protect myself through the practice
        of patience,
    The same effect will not ripen on others.

(51)   *'Then would it not be better to return their harm?'*
No! Retaliation would not protect them;
It would just cause my Bodhisattva vow to
    degenerate
And destroy my practice of patience.

(52)   Since my mind is not a bodily form,
There is no one who can destroy it;
But, because I am strongly attached to my body,
I feel hurt when it is suffering.

(53)   Contempt, harsh words
And unpleasant speech
Do not harm the body;
So why, mind, do you become so angry?

(54)   *'Such slanderous words may cause others to dislike you.'*
Their dislike will not cause me any harm
In this or future lives;
So why should I not want it?

(55)   *'If people dislike you, that might prevent you*
From acquiring wealth or status.'
But I shall lose all my worldly acquisitions when I
    die –
The only thing to remain will be the non-virtue I
    create.

(56)   It would be better for me to die today
Than to live a long life filled with non-virtue;
And, even if I have a long life,
I shall still have to face the suffering of death.

(57)   If one person were to awake from a dream
       In which he had experienced a hundred years of
           happiness,
       And another were to awake from a dream
       In which he had experienced but a brief moment of
           happiness,

(58)   Once awake, the situation would be the same for
           both
       Because neither could ever return to that happiness.
       In the same way, whether our life is long or short,
       At the time of death everything ends just the same.

(59)   Even if I live happily for a long time
       And acquire great wealth and possessions,
       I shall still have to leave this life empty-handed and
           naked,
       As if I had been robbed by a thief.

(60)   *'Even so, acquiring wealth will support your life*
       So that you can purify non-virtue and accumulate merit.'
       But if in acquiring that wealth I generate non-virtues
           such as anger,
       It will be my non-virtue that increases and my merit
           that declines.

(61)   What is the point of a life
       In which we commit only non-virtue?
       Non-virtues are the main cause of our suffering,
       And suffering is the main object to be abandoned!

(62) *'At least you should retaliate when people speak ill of you*
      And cause others to lose their faith in you.'
      In that case, why do I not get angry
      When people speak ill of others?

(63) If, mind, you can forbear such loss of faith
      When it is related to others,
      Why are you not patient when others speak ill of
        you,
      For that is related to the arising of delusions?

(64) Even if someone were to insult or destroy the
        Dharma,
      The holy images or the stupas,
      It would still not be appropriate to get angry with
        them,
      For how could the Three Jewels ever be harmed?

(65) We should also prevent anger arising towards
        anyone
      Who might harm our Spiritual Guide, our friends
        or our relatives
      By seeing that such harm also occurs in dependence
        upon conditions
      In the way that was just explained.

(66) Embodied beings are harmed
      By both animate and inanimate objects;
      So why become angry only with animate ones?
      We should be patient with both types of harm.

(67) If one person causes harm out of ignorance
      And another gets angry with him, also out of
          ignorance,
      Which person is at fault
      And which one is not?

(68) Out of ignorance, previously I committed actions
      That now result in others causing me harm.
      Thus, all the harm I receive is related to my own
          actions,
      So why get angry with others?

(69) Seeing this to be the case,
      I should practise what is meritorious,
      Impelled by the wish that all living beings
      Will develop love for one another.

(70) If, for example, a house caught fire
      And there was a danger of the fire spreading to an
          adjacent house,
      It would be advisable to remove anything, such as
          dry grass,
      That might enable the fire to spread.

(71) In the same way, when those to whom I cling are
          harmed,
      My attachment to them enables the fire of anger to
          spread to me.
      Fearing that this will consume all my merit,
      I should definitely abandon such attachment.

(72)   How fortunate is a person condemned to death
Who is spared with having just his hand cut off;
And how fortunate are we if, instead of the agonies
    of hell,
We have to experience only the sufferings of the
    human realm.

(73)   If we cannot bear the relatively slight suffering
That we have to experience now,
Why do we not refrain from anger,
Which causes the far greater sufferings of hell?

(74)   In the past, because of my attachment to non-
    virtuous actions,
I have endured aeons of torment in the hells and
    elsewhere,
And yet none of that has brought any benefit
Either to myself or to others;

(75)   But now, through enduring comparatively little
    discomfort,
I can accomplish the greatest purpose of all –
To free all living beings from their suffering –
So I should feel only joy at having to endure such
    hardships.

(76)   If someone else develops a mind of joy
Through praising another's good qualities,
Why, mind, do you not praise him too
And experience the same kind of joy?

(77)   I should always rejoice in others' happiness and
           virtue.
        This joy causes my virtues to increase.
        Moreover, it is the cause of delighting the holy
           beings
        And the supreme method for benefiting others.

(78)   Those who are not concerned with others' happiness
        And do not want them to be happy,
        Are like someone who stops paying wages to those
           who work for him,
        Who then experiences many problems.

(79)   When my own good qualities are praised,
        I want others to rejoice in me;
        So why, when others' good qualities are praised,
        Should I not want to rejoice in them?

(80)   Having generated the bodhichitta motivation
        Wishing for all living beings to be happy,
        Why on earth do we not rejoice
        When others find some happiness for themselves?

(81)   If I really wish for living beings to become Buddhas,
        Who are worshipped throughout all worlds,
        Why do I dislike it so
        When others receive a little mundane respect now?

(82)   If someone I was looking after
        And providing for in different ways
        Were to find his own source of livelihood,
        Surely I would be happy, not upset.

(83)   If I begrudge living beings even this,
       How can I wish for them to attain enlightenment?
       Where is the bodhichitta in one who is not happy
       When others receive something good?

(84)   People become angry when someone benefits their
            enemy,
       But, whether their enemy receives benefit or not,
       It is the enemy's own anger that urges him to attack;
       So it is that anger which is to blame, not the
            benefactor.

(85)   Why, by getting angry, do we throw away our merit,
       The faith others have in us, and our other good
            qualities?
       Would it not be better to get angry with anger itself,
       For it brings no benefit to us or to others?

(86)   It is bad enough that you, mind, have no remorse
       For the non-virtues you have committed;
       But why do you compound it
       By being jealous with those who practise virtue?

(87)   The thought that wishes for our enemy to suffer
       Harms only us, through creating non-virtue;
       Understanding this, we should not develop harmful
            thoughts
       Towards anyone, including our enemies.

(88)   And even if your enemy did suffer as you wish,
       How would that benefit you?
       If you say, *'Well, at least it would give me some
            satisfaction'*,
       How can there be a mind lower than that?

86

(89)　Such thoughts are like unbearably sharp hooks
Cast by the fishermen of the delusions, such as
　　anger.
Once caught on them, we shall definitely be boiled
　　alive
In the terrifying cauldrons of the guardians of hell.

(90)　Praise, fame and good reputation
Will not increase my merit or extend my life,
Nor will they give me strength, freedom from
　　illness,
Or any form of physical pleasure.

(91)　Transient pleasures, such as drinking and playing
　　meaningless games,
Are deceptive.
If I understand the real meaning of a human life,
Such things will have no value for me.

(92)　For the sake of fame and reputation,
People give away their wealth and even sacrifice
　　their lives;
But what good can a few dry words do when we
　　die?
To whom can they bring any pleasure?

(93)　When people lose their reputation,
They become despondent, like a child
Who cries when the sandcastle he has built
Is washed away by the tide.

(94) A few short-lived, inanimate sounds
      Can have no intention to praise me.
      'But they are a source of pleasure for the one who praises
          you;
      So you should be happy too.'

(95) Whether someone praises me or others,
      How shall I benefit from their pleasure?
      Since it is entirely in their mind,
      I shall not receive any part of it.

(96) *'But you should be happy because he is happy.'*
      Then I should feel the same way about everyone –
      In which case I should also be happy
      When something pleases my enemy!

(97) Seeking happiness from praise
      Given by friends and others
      Is entirely inappropriate –
      It is completely childish behaviour.

(98) Praise and so forth distract me from virtue,
      Weaken my disillusionment with samsara,
      Cause me to envy others' good qualities,
      And undermine everything that is beneficial.

(99) Therefore, those who conspire
      To prevent me from being praised
      Are really acting to prevent me
      From falling into the lower realms!

(100)   I, who seek liberation, have no need for wealth or a
            good reputation
        For they only keep me bound in samsara;
        So why should I get angry
        With those who free me from this bondage?

(101)   Those who cause me suffering
        Are like Buddhas bestowing their blessings.
        Since they lead me to liberating paths,
        Why should I get angry with them?

(102)   *'Don't they obstruct your virtuous practice?'*
        No! There is no virtuous practice greater than
            patience;
        Therefore, I will never get angry
        With those who cause me suffering.

(103)   If, because of my own shortcomings,
        I do not practise patience with my enemy,
        It is not he, but I, who prevent me from practising
            patience,
        The cause of accumulating merit.

(104)   My enemy is the cause of my accumulating the merit
            of patience
        Because without him there is no patience to practise,
        Whereas with him there is.
        So how does he obstruct my virtuous practice?

(105)   A beggar is not an obstacle
        To people practising giving
        Any more than an Abbot is an obstacle
        To those wishing to ordain.

(106)   Indeed, there are many beggars in this world,
        But people who harm me are extremely rare.
        In fact, if I had not inflicted harm on others in the
            past,
        There would be no one to inflict harm on me now!

(107)   Just as if some treasure were suddenly to appear in
            my house
        Without my making any effort to obtain it,
        I should be delighted to have found an enemy
        Who can help me practise the conduct that leads to
            enlightenment.

(108)   Along with myself, my enemy is the cause of my
            practising patience.
        Therefore, I should first dedicate
        Whatever fruits arise from this practice
        To the person who was a cause of it.

(109)   *'But your enemy has no intention to help you practise*
            patience,
        So why should you venerate him?'
        Then why venerate the holy Dharma
        As a way of practising virtue?

(110)   *'Surely you should not venerate an enemy*
        Who harbours the intention to cause you harm.'
        But if everyone was like a doctor striving to help me,
        When would I ever practise patience?

(111) Thus, because the practice of patience occurs
       In dependence upon those with hateful minds,
       Such people should be venerated just like the holy
           Dharma
       Because they are causes of the practice of patience.

(112) Buddha says that the field of living beings
       Is like the field of enlightened beings,
       For there are many practitioners who, through
           pleasing living beings,
       Have attained the state of perfection, Buddhahood.

(113) Since living beings and enlightened beings are alike
       In that the qualities of a Buddha arise in dependence
           upon them,
       Why do we not show the same respect to living
           beings
       As we do to the enlightened beings?

(114) They are not equal with regard to their realizations;
       But, because living beings have the good quality
       Of helping to produce the same result, Buddhahood,
       They are equal in the sense of also being a field of
           merit.

(115) Whatever merit there is in venerating one with
           limitless love
       Is due to the greatness of all living beings,
       And whatever merit there is in having faith in the
           Buddhas
       Is due to the greatness of the Buddhas.

(116)   Thus, they are said to be equal because being
            respectful to both
         Leads to the attainment of the state of Buddhahood;
         But because living beings do not possess limitless
            good qualities,
         They are not actually equal to Buddhas.

(117)   The unique qualities of a Buddha are so extensive
         That any being in whom even a small fraction of
            them appears
         Is worthy of veneration that would not be
            adequately expressed
         Even by offering them everything in the three
            worlds.

(118)   Therefore, because they share in giving rise
         To the supreme state of Buddhahood,
         At least from this point of view
         It is suitable to venerate living beings.

(119)   Moreover, besides pleasing living beings,
         What other way is there for us to repay
         Those supreme, unchanging friends
         Who bestow immeasurable benefit?

(120)   By benefiting these living beings, I can repay
            Buddha,
         Who many times gave up his life and entered the
            deepest hell for their sake.
         Therefore, even if they inflict great harm on me,
         I will always treat them respectfully and with a good
            heart.

(121)   If Buddhas, who are far superior to me,
Disregard their own bodies for the sake of living
    beings,
Why do I act out of foolish pride
And not behave as if I were a servant of others?

(122)   Buddhas are delighted when living beings are happy
And displeased when they are harmed;
So it follows that, when I please or harm living
    beings,
It is the same as pleasing or harming all the
    Buddhas.

(123)   If we harm a child,
There is no way to please its mother.
In the same way, if we harm any living being,
There is no way to please the compassionate
    Buddhas.

(124)   Therefore, since I have caused harm to living beings,
Which has displeased the compassionate Buddhas,
Today I confess individually all these non-virtues –
Please, O Compassionate Ones, forgive me for
    offending you so.

(125)   From now on, to delight the Tathagatas,
I will definitely become like a servant to all living
    beings.
Even if people kick me and humiliate me,
I will please the Buddhas by not retaliating.

(126)   There is no doubt that the compassionate Buddhas
        Have completed exchanging self with all living
            beings.
        Thus, the nature of living beings is the very nature of
            the Buddhas,
        So we should afford them the same respect.

(127)   Practising in this way pleases all the Buddhas,
        Is a perfect method for accumulating good fortune,
        And gives me the ability to dispel the sufferings of
            the world.
        Therefore, I should always practise the three types of
            patience.

(128)   If, for example, a king's minister
        Were to cause harm to many people,
        Far-sighted people would not retaliate
        Even if they were able to do so

(129)   Because they would see that he was not alone
        But was supported by the might of the king.
        In the same way, we should not retaliate
        To those who cause us a little harm,

(130)   Because they are supported by the compassionate
            Buddhas –
        And by the guardians of hell!
        Therefore, we should be like the subjects of a
            powerful king
        And try to please other living beings.

(131) Even if such a king were to get angry,
He would not be able to subject me to the sufferings
of hell,
Which is what I shall experience
If I harm other beings.

(132) And, no matter how benevolent that king might be,
He could not bestow upon me the attainment of
Buddhahood,
Which is what I shall experience
If I please other beings.

(133) Why can I not see that my eventual attainment of
Buddhahood,
And my success, good reputation
And prosperity in this life,
All come from pleasing other living beings?

(134) Even while I remain in samsara,
Through patience I shall attain beautiful forms,
Good health, reputation, very long lives
And even the extensive happiness of a chakravatin
king!

This concludes the sixth chapter of *Guide to the Bodhisattva's Way of Life*, entitled 'Relying upon Patience'.

Chapter 7:

Relying upon Effort

When I find myself assailed by a host of delusions,
I will oppose them in a thousand ways.
Like a lion among a group of foxes,
I will not allow myself to be harmed by delusions.

Relying upon Effort

(1)   With the practice of patience I should train in effort
       Because the fruit of enlightenment depends upon it.
       Just as a candle flame cannot move without wind,
       So the collections of wisdom and merit cannot grow
            without effort.

(2)   Effort is a mind that delights in virtue.
       Its opponents are the laziness of indolence,
       The laziness of being attracted to non-virtuous actions
       And the laziness of discouragement.

(3)   The laziness of indolence develops
       When, through being attracted to worldly pleasures,
       And particularly to the pleasures of sleep,
       We fail to become disillusioned with the sufferings
            of samsara.

(4)   Why do we not realize that while we are caught
In the snare of delusions such as laziness,
We are trapped in the net of samsara
And held within the jaws of the Lord of Death?

(5)   If I check carefully, I can see that the Lord of Death
Is systematically slaughtering everyone;
Yet still I am not concerned about my death,
Just like an animal unconcerned about being
    butchered.

(6)   The Lord of Death is looking for his next victim
So that he can prevent him from travelling the path
    to liberation,
And that victim might well be me;
So how can I just indulge in worldly pleasures?

(7)   The time of death will come quickly,
So accumulate wisdom and merit while you can.
Do not wait until the time of death to abandon
    laziness,
For then it will be too late!

(8)   With some things not yet started
And others half-finished,
The Lord of Death will suddenly strike
And I shall think, 'Oh no, this is the end for me!'

(9)   When I become a victim of the Lord of Death,
My relatives – their eyes red and swollen with
    sorrow
And their faces flushed with tears –
Will finally give up hope.

(10)   Tormented by memories of my previous non-virtues
And hearing the sounds of impending hell,
Out of terror I shall cover myself in excrement!
What shall I be able to do in such a pathetic state?

(11)   If even in this human life I shall experience terror
Like that felt by a fish being cooked alive,
What can be said of the unbearable sufferings of
    hell
That I shall experience as a consequence of my non-
    virtuous actions?

(12)   As a result of the non-virtues I have committed,
I shall be reborn in the hot hells
Where my tender, young flesh will be scalded by
    hot, molten metals;
So how can I remain at ease under the control of
    laziness?

(13)   I wish for higher attainments without having to
    make any effort,
Permanent freedom without having patiently to
    endure any pain,
And to remain like a long-life god while living in
    the jaws of death.
How foolish I am! When death comes, I shall be
    overwhelmed by suffering!

(14)   By depending upon this boat-like human form,
We can cross the great ocean of suffering.
Since such a vessel will be hard to find again,
This is no time to sleep, you fool!

(15)   Why do I forsake the joy of holy Dharma,
Which is a boundless source of happiness,
Just to seek pleasure in distractions and meaningless
    pursuits
That are only causes of suffering?

(16)   Without being discouraged, I should collect wisdom
    and merit
And strive for self-control through mindfulness and
    alertness.
Then I should equalize self and others
And practise exchanging myself with others.

(17)   I should not discourage myself by thinking,
'How shall I ever become enlightened?'
For the Tathagatas, who speak only the truth,
Have said that it can be so.

(18)   It is said that even flies, bees, gnats
And all other insects and animals
Can attain the rare and unsurpassed state of
    enlightenment
Through developing the power of effort;

(19)   So why should I, who am born a human,
And who understand the meaning of spiritual
    paths,
Not attain enlightenment
By following the Bodhisattva's way of life?

(20)   Some people might be discouraged out of fear
Of having to sacrifice their flesh,
But this is due to not understanding
What we should give, or when.

102

(21)   In our previous lives, over countless aeons,
We have been cut, stabbed, burned
And flayed alive innumerable times;
But we have not achieved anything from these
    hardships.

(22)   Yet the hardships we must forbear to attain
    enlightenment
Are insignificant compared to these.
It is like enduring the lesser suffering of surgery
So as to stop much greater pain.

(23)   If doctors have to use unpleasant medical
    treatments
To cure people of their illnesses,
I should be able to forbear a few discomforts
To destroy the many sufferings of samsara.

(24)   But Buddha, the Supreme Physician, does not use
Ordinary treatments such as these;
Rather, he uses extremely gentle methods
To eliminate all the great diseases of the delusions.

(25)   To begin with, Buddha, the Guide, encourages us
To practise giving such things as food.
Later, when we become used to this,
We can gradually learn to give our own flesh.

(26)   When eventually we develop a mind
That regards our body as being just like food,
What discomfort shall we feel
From giving away our flesh?

(27)   The Bodhisattva has abandoned non-virtue and so
          does not experience physical suffering;
       And, because he clearly realizes emptiness, he does
          not experience mental pain.
       By contrast, we are afflicted by wrong conceptions
       And our bodies and minds are harmed by non-
          virtuous actions.

(28)   Because of his merit, the Bodhisattva experiences
          physical happiness,
       And because of his wisdom, mental joy;
       So even if this compassionate one must abide in
          samsara for the sake of others,
       How could he ever be perturbed?

(29)   Through the power of his bodhichitta,
       He purified all his previous non-virtue;
       And because he accumulates vast collections of
          merit and wisdom,
       He is said to surpass the Hearers.

(30)   Having mounted the steed of bodhichitta
       That dispels mental discouragement and physical
          weariness,
       The Bodhisattva travels the path from joy to joy.
       Knowing this, who could ever be discouraged?

(31)   The four powers that assist us in working for the
          benefit of others
       Are the powers of aspiration, self-confidence, joy
          and rejection.
       The power of aspiration is generated by
          contemplating the benefits of virtuous actions
       And developing fear of the cycle of suffering.

104

(32)   Having overcome all three types of laziness,
I should continuously strive to increase my effort
Through aspiration, self-confidence, joy and
    rejection,
And through the force of familiarity and mental
    suppleness.

(33)   In the past, I have accumulated
Countless non-virtuous actions,
Even just one of which can cause me
To experience many aeons of suffering,

(34)   But, because of my laziness,
I have not purified any of these evils
And so I remain as an abode of infinite suffering.
Why does my heart not crack open with fear?

(35)   I need to attain the good qualities of a Bodhisattva
For the sake of myself and others,
But it might take me many aeons
To accomplish just one of these.

(36)   Up to now, I have not familiarized myself
With even a fraction of these good qualities.
How tragic it would be if I were now to waste
This rare and precious rebirth on meaningless
    pursuits!

(37)   Do I have faith and respect in Buddha?
Have I practised his teachings, the Dharma?
Do I rely upon the supreme spiritual friends, the
    Sangha?
Have I fulfilled the wishes of the poor and needy?

(38) Do I give help to those in danger
      Or relief to those who are suffering?
      No! All I have done is experience the discomforts
      Of being in my mother's womb, and all the
          subsequent sufferings.

(39) In my previous lives I held views
      That denied Buddha's teachings
      And, as a result, I am now very poor in spiritual
          realizations.
      Knowing this, how can I give up the practice of
          Dharma?

(40) Buddha, the Able One, has said
      That the root of Dharma is the intention to
          practise it.
      We can generate this intention by meditating
      On the law of karma, or actions and their effects.

(41) All physical suffering and mental unhappiness,
      All the different types of fear,
      And the suffering of being separated from what
          we want
      Arise from non-virtuous actions.

(42) Through committing non-virtuous actions,
      Even though we may wish for happiness
      We shall be pierced by the weapons of suffering
      Wherever we find ourself;

(43)   But, through performing virtuous actions with a
       pure intention,
We shall be sustained by a happiness
That results from that merit,
Wherever we are reborn.

(44)   Those born in Buddha's Pure Land arise from the
       lotus of pure actions performed through receiving
       the light of Conqueror Buddha's blessings.
They are completely pure, uncontaminated by
       delusions, like a lotus unstained by mud.
Nourished by hearing Conqueror Buddha's speech
       directly, they experience supreme inner peace.
All this happiness and goodness is the result of
       virtuous actions, such as the six perfections,
       prayer and dedication.

(45)   By contrast, those born in hell, on the fiery ground of
       red-hot iron, suffer at the hands of the henchmen
       of the Lord of Death,
Who tear open their skin and pour molten copper
       into their bodies
And then, piercing them with flaming swords and
       spears, cut their flesh into hundreds of fragments.
Such sufferings, which are experienced for many
       aeons, are the result of non-virtuous actions.

(46)   Therefore, I should always keep the intention to
       accumulate virtues, not non-virtues,
And put this intention into practice with strong effort.
As mentioned in *Vajradotsa Sutra*,
Whatever Dharma practice I study, I should
       complete it with strong confidence.

(47) First, I should examine what is to be done,
To see whether I can do it or not.
If I am unable to do it, I should not start it;
But, once I start something, I should never turn back.

(48) Otherwise this habit will carry into my future lives
And my non-virtue and suffering will continue to
increase.
Moreover, other virtuous actions will take a long
time to accomplish
And will yield only meagre results.

(49) I should maintain self-confidence in three things:
My Dharma practice, my Dharma activities and
overcoming my own delusions.
I should encourage myself by thinking, 'I alone
will lead all living beings to the happiness of
enlightenment',
And in this way sustain my self-confidence in these
three things.

(50) Unlike me, worldly beings are powerless.
Being under the control of delusion and karma,
They are unable to make their lives meaningful.
Therefore, I will practise virtue for their sake.

(51) How can I sit and do nothing
While others waste their lives on meaningless tasks?
Although it might seem like self-importance,
I should act out of self-confidence, which is quite
different from self-importance.

(52)   If a snake lies dying on the ground,
       Crows will act like brave eagles and attack it.
       In the same way, if my self-confidence is weak,
       Even the slightest adversity will be able to
           harm me.

(53)   If, out of laziness, I give up trying,
       How shall I ever attain liberation in such a feeble
           state?
       But if, out of self-confidence, I generate effort,
       It will be difficult for even the greatest adversity to
           harm me.

(54)   Therefore, with a steadfast mind
       I will overcome all downfalls
       For, if I am defeated by a downfall,
       My wish to triumph over all obstacles will be but
           a joke.

(55)   'I will conquer all obstacles,
       And none shall conquer me.'
       Thus I, who will become a Conqueror,
       Will practise with self-confidence.

(56)   Anyone who is governed by the view of
           self-importance
       Is under the influence of delusion, not
           self-confidence.
       Such a person has succumbed to the enemy of the
           self-important view,
       Whereas one with self-confidence has not.

(57)   Those who are inflated by the deluded view of
           self-importance
       Will be reborn in the lower realms;
       And, if they later take rebirth in a human form,
       They will be poor and miserable, like slaves eating
           others' food.

(58)   Stupid, ugly and feeble, they will be despised by
           everyone.
       So-called 'tough people' who are puffed up with
           pride
       Are also counted among the self-important –
       Who could be more pathetic than they are?

(59)   By contrast, whoever develops the self-confidence
           to conquer the enemy of the self-important view
       Is a self-confident one who is a true conquering
           hero;
       And whoever completely eradicates the enemy of
           the self-important view
       Will be able to fulfil the temporary wishes of
           living beings and bestow upon them the fruit of
           enlightenment.

(60)   When I find myself assailed by a host of delusions,
       I will oppose them in a thousand ways.
       Like a lion among a group of foxes,
       I will not allow myself to be harmed by delusions.

(61)   Just as people protect their eyes
       When in dangerous situations,
       So, whenever there is a danger of the delusions,
       I will protect myself from their influence.

(62) It would be far better for me to be burned to death
Or to have my head cut off
Than it would be for me ever to submit
To the enemy of the delusions.

(63) Like a Bodhisattva, I should long to work for others
With the same enthusiasm as that possessed by
someone
Who thoroughly enjoys playing a game.
I should never tire, but experience uninterrupted joy.

(64) Although it is uncertain whether the result will be
happiness or suffering,
Worldly people still work hard to make themselves
happy;
So why do we not derive joy from the practice of
Dharma,
Which definitely results in happiness?

(65) I have a strong wish to pursue objects of desire,
Which, like honey on a razor's edge, give no real
satisfaction;
But it would be far better to develop a strong wish to
pursue virtuous actions,
Which result in the everlasting happiness of
liberation from all suffering.

(66) Therefore, to complete the virtuous actions
mentioned above,
I will engage in them with the same enthusiasm
As that with which an elephant, tormented by the
heat of the day,
Plunges into a cool, refreshing pool.

(67)   If I become weak or tired, I should stop what I am
      doing
And continue with it once I have rested.
When I have done something well, I should not be
      attached,
But move on to what needs to be done next.

(68)   Just as a seasoned warrior on the battlefront
Approaches the enemy's weapons with care,
So will I protect myself from the weapons of the
      delusions
And bind these enemies so that I can destroy them.

(69)   If someone drops his weapon during a battle,
Out of fear he will immediately pick it up again.
Likewise, if I ever lose the weapon of mindfulness,
I will recall the sufferings of hell and out of fear
      restore it straightaway.

(70)   Just as a little poison will spread throughout the
      body
With the circulation of the blood,
So, given an opportunity,
The delusions will spread throughout my mind.

(71)   A Dharma practitioner should practise as attentively
As a person would walk if he were forced to carry a
      jar brimming with oil,
Fearful in the knowledge that, if he spilled just one
      drop,
The tormentor behind him would slay him with a
      sword.

(72) Therefore, just as I would quickly jump up
      If a snake were to crawl into my lap,
      So, whenever sleep or laziness threaten,
      I will swiftly remove them from my mind.

(73) Each time faults such as delusions arise,
      I will thoroughly chastise myself
      And then focus for a long time
      On the determination not to let that happen again.

(74) In this way, in all situations
      I will acquaint myself with mindfulness –
      Sincerely and purely practising Dharma
      So that I can protect myself and others from
          suffering.

(75) To ensure that I have the strength for all of this,
      Before I commence I will recall
      The instructions on conscientiousness
      And rise to these tasks with suppleness of body
          and mind.

(76) Just as a piece of cotton moving back and forth
      Is controlled by the movement of the wind,
      So with my body, speech and mind controlled by
          the joy of effort
      I will swiftly accomplish all realizations.

This concludes the seventh chapter of *Guide to the Bodhisattva's Way of Life*, entitled 'Relying upon Effort'.

Chapter 8:

Relying upon Mental Stabilization

When shall I withdraw into the forest
And live among the trees
With birds and deer who say nothing unpleasant
But are a joy to live with?

CHAPTER 8

Relying upon Mental Stabilization

(1)   Having generated effort in this way,
       I should place my mind in concentration;
       For a person whose mind is distracted
       Is trapped within the fangs of the delusions.

(2)   Distractions do not arise for those
       Who abide in physical and mental solitude.
       Therefore, I should forsake the worldly life
       And abandon all disturbing thoughts.

(3)   Attachment to people, possessions and reputation
       Prevent me from forsaking the worldly life.
       To abandon these obstacles,
       I should contemplate as follows.

(4)   Realizing that delusions are thoroughly destroyed
       By superior seeing conjoined with tranquil abiding,
       I should first strive to attain tranquil abiding
       By gladly forsaking attachment to worldly life.

(5)   I, who am decaying moment by moment, have
          attachment to others
      Who are also decaying moment by moment.
      As a result of this, I shall not be able to see
      Pure, attractive objects for thousands of lifetimes.

(6)   If I do not see someone whom I find attractive,
      I become unhappy and cannot place my mind in
          concentration;
      Yet, when I do see that person, I find no satisfaction
      But am just as tormented by attachment as I was
          before.

(7)   Having strong attachment to other living beings
      Obstructs the correct view of emptiness,
      Prevents renunciation for samsara,
      And causes great sorrow at the time of death.

(8)   While we preoccupy ourself with the things of this
          life,
      Our whole life passes without any meaning.
      For the sake of impermanent friends and relatives,
      We neglect the Dharma that leads to permanent
          liberation.

(9)   By behaving in such a childish way,
      We definitely create the causes of lower rebirth.
      Since worldly beings lead us to unfortunate states,
      What is the point of relying on them?

(10) One moment they are friends,
The next moment they become enemies;
And even while they are enjoying themselves, they
become angry –
How unreliable worldly beings are!

(11) If I tell them about something that is meaningful,
they become angry
And even try to prevent me from engaging in that
meaningful action;
Yet if I do not listen to what they say, they become
angry with that
And in so doing create the causes of lower rebirth!

(12) The childish are jealous of anyone superior to them,
Competitive with their equals, and arrogant towards
their inferiors.
They are conceited when praised but get angry if
criticized.
There is never any benefit in being attached to
them.

(13) As a result of associating with the childish,
We naturally engage in unwholesome actions
Such as praising ourself, disparaging others
And discussing the importance of worldly
pleasures.

(14) The relationships I have made with the childish
Have been completely deceptive,
For the childish have done nothing to fulfil my
wishes
And I have done nothing to fulfil theirs.

(15)   Therefore, I should withdraw to a great distance
          from the childish.
        If I should subsequently meet them, I should
          please them by being happy
        And, without becoming too close,
        Act in agreeable ways according to convention.

(16)   Just as a bee takes pollen from a flower,
        So should I gather only what I need to sustain my
          practice
        And then, without clinging, return to abide in
          solitude
        As if I had never met anyone.

(17)   If people think I have many possessions,
        They will respect me and like me;
        But if I harbour this kind of pride,
        I shall experience terrible fears after I die.

(18)   O thoroughly confused mind,
        For as many objects as you accumulate,
        You will have to endure a thousand times more
          suffering
        Because of your attachment to them.

(19)   Thus, because objects of attachment give rise to
          fear,
        The wise should not become attached,
        But remain firm in the understanding
        That by their very nature these things are to be
          left behind.

(20)   Even if I have acquired many possessions,
Fame, and a good reputation,
None of these things
Can go with me when I die.

(21)   Why am I unhappy when someone criticizes me
And happy when I am praised?
Both criticism and praise are just empty words,
Like echoes in an empty cave.

(22)   Living beings have so many different inclinations
That even Buddha is unable to satisfy them all;
So what chance do I, an ordinary confused being,
    have?
Therefore, I should give up the wish to associate
    with worldly beings.

(23)   They look down on those who do not have wealth
And despise those who do.
How can people who are so hard to get along with
Ever see anything but faults in me?

(24)   Whenever their wishes are not fulfilled,
The childish become unhappy.
This is why the Tathagatas have advised us
Not to associate with them.

(25)   When shall I withdraw into the forest
And live among the trees
With birds and deer who say nothing unpleasant
But are a joy to live with?

(26) Or dwell in a cave or an empty shrine,
      Or abide beneath the trees,
      With a mind unfettered by attachment,
      Which never turns to look back?

(27) When shall I live in a place that no one calls
          'mine' –
      A place that is naturally open and spacious,
      Where I can act freely and do as I wish,
      Without any attachment to body or possessions?

(28) With just a few possessions, such as a begging bowl
      And clothes that no one else wants,
      I shall be free from any danger of thieves and
          robbers.
      In this way, I should live without grasping onto 'I'
          or 'mine'.

(29) I should withdraw to a burial ground
      And meditate on the impermanence of my body
      By thinking that it is really no different from a
          dead body,
      For both are decaying moment by moment.

(30) It might happen that, when I die,
      My body will decay quickly and emit an odour so
          foul
      That not even foxes will want to come near it!
      I should happily accept that such things could
          happen.

(31)   If this body, which is one unit,
Will break into separate pieces
Of flesh and bone,
What can be said of my relationships?

(32)   At birth I was born alone
And at death I shall have to die alone.
Since I cannot share these sufferings with others,
What use are friends who prevent me from
      practising virtue?

(33)   Just as people who travel have no attachment
To a guest house where they stay for just one night,
So should I not develop attachment to this body,
Which is the guest house for just one rebirth.

(34)   Before such time as this body of mine
Is borne aloft by four pallbearers
And worldly beings grieve my passing,
I will withdraw to the solitude of the forest.

(35)   Encountering neither friends nor enemies,
My body will remain in complete solitude.
If I am already counted among the dead,
There will be no one to mourn me when I die.

(36)   Then, with no one around me
Grieving or planning harm,
Who will there be to distract me
From my recollection of holy Buddha?

(37)   Therefore, I will dwell alone
In a quiet and peaceful place.
Happy, contented and with no worries,
I will strive to pacify all distractions.

(38)   Having given up all other desires
And being motivated solely by bodhichitta,
I will strive to attain single-pointed concentration
And control my mind by recollecting the meaning
     of emptiness.

(39)   Deluded desires give rise to misfortune
In both this and future lives.
In this life they cause injury, incarceration and
     death,
And in the next the sufferings of the lower realms.

(40)   For the sake of acquiring a sexual partner,
People send messages through go-betweens
And, disregarding any harm to their reputation,
Commit all manner of non-virtue.

(41)   Although we engage in harmful actions
And even sacrifice all our wealth for them,
What is the real nature of these bodies
That we like so much to embrace?

(42)   They are nothing other than skeletons
That are neither autonomous nor inherently
     existent.
Rather than being so desirous and attached to
     them,
Why do I not strive to pass beyond sorrow
     instead?

(43)   When we are very attached to someone,
        We want to see their face again and again;
        But, whether we see their face or not,
        The real face always remains covered with skin.

(44)   If we were to remove that skin,
        We would realize that they are not an object of
            desire
        But an object of aversion;
        So why do we develop attachment for others'
            bodies?

(45)   Although we jealously guard our lover from others'
            advances,
        The Lord of Death will take him from us
        And his body will be burned or buried in the
            ground;
        So what is the point of our jealousy and attachment?

(46)   Others' bodies to which we are very attached
        Are just collections of flesh and bone.
        At any moment, they could be destroyed by the
            Lord of Death;
        So why develop attachment to them?

(47)   When we see a human corpse, which is a mere
            collection of flesh and bone,
        We develop fear even though it does not move;
        So why are we not fearful of living bodies, which
            are also just collections of flesh and bone
        Moving here and there like zombies?

(48)   Since both dead bodies and living bodies
Are mere collections of flesh and bone,
Why am I attracted to living bodies but not to dead
    ones?
Thinking in this way, I should stop attachment to
    others' bodies.

(49)   Both saliva and urine come from the same source –
The intake of fluids into the body –
So why is it that we like saliva when kissing
But have no desire for urine?

(50)   Although cotton is also soft to touch,
You find no sexual pleasure in a pillow.
Rather, you think the body does not emit foul
    smells –
O desirous mind, you are so confused about what
    is unclean!

(51)   Just as we sometimes get angry at other people,
Why don't we also get angry at pillows?
For, although they too are soft to touch,
We cannot copulate with them!

(52)   We might feel that what we are attracted to is not
    impure;
And yet we want to copulate with others' bodies,
Which are just cages of bone tied together with
    muscles
And plastered over with the mud of flesh!

(53)   We have enough impurities of our own
That we constantly have to contend with;
So why, out of an obsession with the unclean,
Do we desire other bags of filth?

(54)   *'It is the flesh that I enjoy.'*
If this is what you like to see and touch,
Why do you not want it in its natural state –
When it is devoid of mind?

(55)   Any mind that you desire
Can be neither seen nor touched,
And anything you can see or touch cannot be mind;
So why engage in meaningless copulation?

(56)   Perhaps it is not so strange
That you do not realize others' bodies are impure,
But it is very strange
That you do not realize your own is.

(57)   If your main interest is in attractive forms,
Why do you not prefer to touch such things
As beautiful young flowers
Rather than desiring others' bodies, which are just
    cages of filth?

(58)   If you do not want to touch a place
Covered with impurities such as vomit,
Why do you want to touch the body
From which these impurities come?

127

(59)   If you are not attached to what is unclean,
Why do you embrace others' bodies,
Which come from impure blood and sperm
Within an unclean womb?

(60)   You have no desire for the body of an insect,
       however small,
That emerges from a pile of dung;
So why do you desire a gross, impure body
That is produced from thirty-six impure
       substances?

(61)   Not only do you not disparage
The impurity of your own body,
But, out of attachment to what is unclean,
You desire other bags of filth!

(62)   Even pure medicinal herbs
And delicately cooked rice or vegetables
Will defile the ground on which they land
If they are spat out after having been in the
       mouth.

(63)   Although the impurity of the body is obvious,
If you still have doubts, go to a burial ground
And reflect on the impurity of the corpses
That have been abandoned there.

(64)   Once you have understood
That, when the skin is removed,
The body gives rise to great aversion,
How can you ever derive pleasure from it again?

(65)   The fragrance of another's body comes from other
          sources,
       Such as the sandalwood with which it is anointed;
       So why are you attracted to a body
       Because of scents that are not its own?

(66)   Since in its natural state the body smells foul,
       Would it not be better to have no attachment for it?
       Why do those who crave the meaningless things of
          this world
       Anoint this body with perfume?

(67)   If the scent comes from perfume, such as
          sandalwood,
       How can it come from the body?
       Why be attached to others
       Because of a scent that is not theirs?

(68)   When left naked in its natural state,
       The body is hideous, with long hair and nails,
       Foul-smelling, yellowing teeth
       And a pervasive stench of dirt.

(69)   Putting so much effort into beautifying it
       Is just like polishing a sword that will be used to
          harm you.
       It seems the whole world is pervaded by this
          madness
       Because people believe beauty is only external.

(70) Having contemplated the piles of bones in the burial
     ground,
     Once we turn our mind elsewhere
     And see graveyard cities full of moving bones,
     How can we find pleasure in them?

(71) Furthermore, we do not come to enjoy others'
     bodies
     Without acquiring material possessions.
     We exhaust ourself in non-virtuous activities to
     gather these,
     Only to experience suffering in this life and the
     lower realms in the next.

(72) When we are young, we do not have the resources to
     support a partner;
     And later we are so busy that there is no time to
     enjoy ourself.
     When at last we have accumulated the resources we
     need,
     We are too old to indulge our desires!

(73) Some, under the influence of desire, work like
     slaves.
     They tire themselves out working long days
     And, when they return home in the evening,
     Their exhausted bodies collapse like corpses.

(74) Some have to experience the disruptions of travel
     Or suffer from being far from home.
     Although they long to be close to their partners,
     They do not see them for years at a time.

(75)   Some, confused about how to earn what they desire,
        Effectively sell themselves to others.
        Even then they do not get what they want
        But are driven without meaning by the needs of
            others.

(76)   Then there are those who sell themselves into
            servitude
        And work for others without any freedom.
        They live in lonely, desolate places
        Where their children are born with only trees for
            shelter.

(77)   Deceived by desire, people become fools.
        Some think, 'I need money to support my life',
        And, although they fear for their lives, go off to war;
        While others enslave themselves for the sake of
            profit!

(78)   Some, as a consequence of their desires,
        Suffer cuts to their bodies
        Or are stabbed, impaled
        Or even burned.

(79)   We should realize that a preoccupation with wealth
            leads to endless problems
        Because acquiring it, protecting it and losing it all
            involve pain.
        Those who allow themselves to become distracted
            out of attachment to wealth
        Will find no opportunity to escape from the miseries
            of samsara.

(80) People attached to a worldly life
Experience many such problems, and for little
reward.
They are like a horse forced to pull a cart,
Who can grab only an occasional mouthful of grass
to eat.

(81) Those who are driven by uncontrolled desires
Waste this precious freedom and endowment, so
hard to find,
For the sake of a few petty rewards that are in no
way rare,
For even animals can obtain them.

(82) Our objects of desire will definitely perish,
And then we shall fall into the lower realms.
If we consider all the hardships we have endured
since beginningless time
In pursuing meaningless worldly pleasures,

(83) We could have attained the state of a Buddha
For a fraction of the difficulty!
Worldly beings experience much greater suffering
than those who follow the path to enlightenment –
And yet they do not attain enlightenment as a result!

(84) If we consider the sufferings of hell and so on,
We shall see that the discomforts endured by
worldly people in this life –
Such as those caused by weapons, poison, enemies
or treacherous places –
Bear no comparison in their severity.

(85)   Thus, having become disillusioned with worldly
             desires,
         We should generate the wish to abide in solitude.
         Fortunate ones stroll in quiet and peaceful places,
         Far away from all conflict and objects of delusion.

(86)   Cooled by flower-scented moonlight
         And fanned by peaceful, silent breezes,
         They abide joyfully without distraction,
         With their minds focused on benefiting others.

(87)   They dwell for as long as they wish
         In empty houses, beneath trees, or in remote
             caves.
         Having abandoned the pain of clinging to and
             guarding possessions,
         They live independently, free from all cares.

(88)   They live freely without attachment
         And unbound by any relationships.
         Even the most powerful humans and gods
         Cannot find a life as contented and happy as this!

(89)   Thus, having contemplated
         The good qualities of solitude,
         I should completely pacify all disturbing
             conceptions
         And meditate on bodhichitta.

(90)   First, I should apply myself to meditation
         On the equality of self and others.
         Because we are all equal in wanting to experience
             happiness and avoid suffering,
         I should cherish all beings as I do myself.

(91)   Although there are many different parts of the body,
such as the arms and the legs,
We protect all these parts as equally as we protect
the body itself.
In a similar way, although there are many different
living beings,
I should cherish them all as equally as I cherish
myself.

(92)   The suffering I experience
Does not harm others,
But I find it hard to bear
Because I cherish myself.

(93)   Likewise, the suffering of others
Does not harm me,
But, if I cherish others,
I shall find their suffering hard to bear.

(94)   Therefore, I should dispel others' suffering
Simply because it is suffering, just like mine;
And I should bring happiness to others
Simply because they are living beings, just like me.

(95)   If both I and others
Are the same in that we wish for happiness,
What is so special about me
That I work only for my own happiness?

(96)   And if both I and others
Are the same in that we wish to avoid suffering,
What is so special about me
That I protect myself but not others?

(97)   But why should I protect others
         If their suffering does me no harm?
         If we cherish only others, we find their suffering
             hard to bear;
         So we definitely need to protect them.

(98)   It is not a wrong conception to think
         That it will be I who experiences the future suffering,
         Because it will not be another person who dies
         And yet another who is reborn.

(99)   *'Surely, whenever there is suffering,*
         It should be dispelled by whoever is experiencing it.'
         Then, since the suffering of the foot is not the hand's,
         Why should the hand help to alleviate it?

(100)   We alleviate the suffering of the foot with the hand
         Because it is a specific method to relieve this pain.
         It is also incorrect to grasp at an independent self
             and others –
         Such grasping should be completely abandoned.

(101)   Things that we call 'continuums' or 'collections',
         Such as rosaries or armies, are falsely existent.
         Thus, there is no independent possessor of suffering,
         For who is there who has control over it?

(102)   Since there is no independent possessor of suffering,
         There is no real difference between my own and
             others' suffering.
         Thus, we should dispel all suffering simply because
             it is painful –
         Why cling to false distinctions with such certainty?

(103)   *'There is no need to dispel everyone else's suffering!'*
        This is not a valid argument.
        If my suffering should be dispelled, so should
            everyone else's;
        And if others' suffering should not be dispelled,
            neither should mine.

(104)   *'But such compassion will bring me suffering,*
        So why should I strive to develop it?'
        How can compassion bring suffering?
        It is the very nature of a peaceful mind!

(105)   If, through one person experiencing relatively little
            suffering,
        The infinite sufferings of living beings can be
            eliminated,
        A kind-hearted Bodhisattva will gladly endure it
        And delight in working for others.

(106)   Thus, although the Bodhisattva Supushpachandra
            understood
        That he would suffer at the hands of the king,
        He did not seek to avoid his own death
        But instead released many others from their suffering.

(107)   Because one whose mind is acquainted with the
            equality of self and others
        Derives great joy from relieving the suffering of
            others,
        For their sakes, he or she would happily enter the
            deepest hell,
        Just like a wild goose plunging into a refreshing
            lotus pool.

(108)   The ocean of joy that will arise
        When all living beings are liberated
        Is everything I wish for –
        So why should I wish for my solitary liberation?

(109)   But although I work for the benefit of others,
        I should do so without pride or pretension.
        Moved only by the joy of benefiting others,
        I should not hope for any reward.

(110)   And just as I protect myself
        From anything unpleasant, however small,
        So should I act towards others
        With a compassionate and caring mind.

(111)   Although there is no I there,
        Through the force of familiarity
        I cling to an I within a body
        That arose from the drops of others' sperm
            and blood.

(112)   In the same way, why can I not
        Identify 'I' with the bodies of others?
        Equally, I should not find it hard
        To identify 'other' with my own body.

(113)   Seeing the faults of cherishing myself
        And the many good qualities of cherishing others,
        I should completely forsake self-cherishing
        And become familiar with cherishing others.

(114)   Just as I regard the hands and so forth
        As limbs of my body,
        So should I regard all living beings
        As limbs of a living whole.

(115) Through the force of familiarity, I generate a mind
That grasps at I with respect to this non-self-existent
body;
So why, through familiarity with cherishing others,
Should I not develop a mind that grasps at I with
respect to others' bodies?

(116) Although I work for others in this way,
I should not develop pride or pretension;
And, just as when I feed myself,
I should hope for nothing in return.

(117) Therefore, just as I protect myself
From anything unpleasant, however small,
So should I become familiar with
A compassionate and caring mind towards others.

(118) Out of his great compassion,
Arya Avalokiteshvara even blessed his own name
To relieve living beings from the fear of
self-cherishing;
So I should recite his name mantra to receive his
blessings.

(119) Do not turn away from learning to cherish others
because it is difficult.
For example, a person's lover may once have been
her enemy, the mere sound of whose name
induced fear;
But now through familiarity she cherishes him
And becomes unhappy when he is not around.

(120) Thus, whoever wants to swiftly protect
Both themselves and others
Should practise this holy secret
Of exchanging self with others.

(121) Because we have attachment for our body,
Even a small object of fear frightens us greatly;
So who would not revile as an enemy
Cherishing this body, which is the source of that
fear?

(122) Out of our wish to find remedies
For the body's hunger, thirst, and sickness,
We kill birds, fish, and other animals
And even resort to attacking people!

(123) Sometimes for money or other possessions
We might even kill our father or mother,
Or steal the property of a spiritual community,
And as a consequence burn in the fires of hell.

(124) Who with wisdom would cherish oneself
Or grasp at this body?
We should view the self-cherishing mind as a foe
And despise it accordingly.

(125) 'If I give this to others, what shall I have to enjoy?'
Such self-cherishing is the mind of a hungry spirit.
'If I enjoy this, what shall I have to give to others?'
Such cherishing of others is the mind of the
enlightened ones.

(126) If we harm others for the sake of our own
    happiness,
We shall suffer the torments of the lower realms;
But if we are harmed for the sake of others'
    happiness,
We shall experience the happiness of higher
    rebirth.

(127) If we hold ourself in high esteem, we shall be
    reborn in the lower realms
And later, as a human, experience low status and a
    foolish mind;
But if we transfer this esteem to others, we shall be
    reborn in fortunate realms,
Command respect, and enjoy good company and
    pleasant surroundings.

(128) If we use others for our own selfish means,
We shall experience servitude ourself;
But if we use ourself for the sake of others,
We shall enjoy high status and pleasing forms.

(129) All the happiness there is in this world
Arises from wishing others to be happy,
And all the suffering there is in this world
Arises from wishing ourself to be happy.

(130) But what need is there to speak at length?
The childish work only for themselves,
Whereas the Buddhas work only for others –
Just look at the difference between them!

(131)   If we do not exchange our happiness
For the suffering of others,
We shall not attain the state of a Buddha
And even in samsara there will be no happiness.

(132)   Never mind what will happen in future lives;
With employees not providing adequate service
Or employers not giving proper reward,
Even our wishes in this life will remain unfulfilled.

(133)   By not cherishing others, we lose the excellent
qualities of our human life
That allow us to attain happiness both now and in
the future;
And if we actually inflict harm on others,
Out of ignorance we shall bring unbearable
suffering upon ourself.

(134)   If all the torment in this world –
All mental fear and physical pain –
Arise from cherishing oneself,
What use is this fearful spirit to us?

(135)   Without destroying fire,
We cannot stop being burned;
Likewise, without destroying self-cherishing,
We cannot stop experiencing suffering.

(136)   Therefore, to eliminate my pain
And pacify the suffering of others,
I will give myself completely to others
And consider them as precious as I now consider
myself to be.

(137) I completely dedicate myself to the happiness of
   others.
From now on, mind, you must understand this
   clearly
And not think of anything
Other than benefiting all living beings.

(138) Because my eyes and so forth are now at the
   disposal of others,
I should not use them for my own purpose;
Nor should I use them in any way
That is contrary to the welfare of others.

(139) Being principally concerned for others,
I will take anything
That I regard as belonging to myself
And use it to benefit them.

(140) Putting myself in the place of those who are lower
   than, equal to, and higher than me,
And then regarding my former self as 'other',
With my mind free from the crippling conception
   of doubt
I should meditate on jealousy, competitiveness
   and pride.

(141) 'He is honoured, but I am not.
I do not have the wealth he has.
He is praised, but I am despised.
He is happy, but I suffer.

(142) 'I have much heavy work to do,
       While he remains comfortably at rest.
       His reputation has spread throughout the world,
       But all I am known for is my lack of good qualities.

(143) 'But what do you mean, "I have no good qualities?"
       I have many such qualities.
       In comparison with many, he is inferior,
       While there are many to whom I am superior.

(144) 'My morals, views, and so on degenerate
       Through the force of my delusions, not because I
          want them to.
       You, Bodhisattva, should help us regenerate them
          in any way that you can,
       And willingly forbear any hardships you might
          encounter in doing so.

(145) 'But he does nothing to help us,
       So why does he make us feel so insignificant?
       What use are his so-called good qualities to us?
       He never uses them for our benefit!

(146) 'Not only does he have no compassion
       For beings such as us dwelling within the jaws of
          the lower realms;
       Externally he displays pride in his own good
          qualities
       And prefers to contend with the wise.'

(147)   'This Bodhisattva is regarded as my equal,
But so that I might outshine him
I will acquire wealth and reputation,
And defeat him in debate.

(148)   'I will proclaim my own good qualities to the whole
        world
By whatever means I can,
But I will make sure that no one ever hears
Of any good qualities he might possess.

(149)   'I will hide my own faults but make his known.
I will be venerated by others but ensure that he is
        not.
I will acquire a great deal of material wealth
And encourage others to honour me, but not him.

(150)   'For a long time, I will take pleasure
In seeing him be humiliated.
I will make him the laughing stock of all
And an object of ridicule and blame.'

(151)   'It is said that this deluded being
Is vying to be my equal,
But how can he compare with me in learning or
        wisdom,
Or in looks, status, or wealth?

(152)   'When others hear of my good qualities
As they are proclaimed to the world,
May they experience so much delight
That their hair pores tingle with excitement.

(153) 'And as for whatever he owns,
       Since he is supposed to be working for us,
       We will allow him just what he needs
       And take the remainder by force for ourselves.

(154) 'Thus, may his happiness decline,
       While we continue to burden him with our
             problems.'
       Countless times in samsaric rebirths,
       This self-cherishing attitude has caused me harm.

(155) O mind, because you wish to benefit yourself,
       All the hard work you have done
       For countless aeons in samsara
       Has resulted only in suffering.

(156) Therefore, I will definitely engage
       In working for the benefit of others;
       And because Buddha's teachings are non-deceptive,
       I shall experience excellent results in the future.

(157) If in the past I had practised
       Exchanging myself with others,
       I would not now be in this situation –
       Devoid of the excellent happiness and bliss of
             Buddhahood.

(158) Just as I am familiar with developing the thought 'I',
             'I',
       When perceiving my body, which arose from others'
             sperm and blood,
       So should I become familiar with developing the
             thought 'I', 'I',
       When perceiving others' bodies.

(159)   Examining myself thoroughly
        To make sure I am working for others,
        I will take whatever I possess
        And use it to benefit them.

(160)   I am happy but others are sad;
        I have a high position but others are lowly;
        I benefit myself but not others –
        Why am I not jealous of myself?

(161)   I must give my happiness to others
        And take their suffering upon myself instead.
        I should constantly examine my behaviour for faults
        By asking, 'Why am I acting in this way?'

(162)   If others do something wrong,
        I will transform it into a fault of my own;
        But if I cause even the slightest harm to others,
        I will declare it openly in the presence of many.

(163)   I should spread the fame of others farther,
        So that it completely outshines my own;
        And, regarding myself as a lowly servant,
        Employ myself in the service of all.

(164)   Being full of faults, I should not praise myself
        Just because of some superficial good quality.
        I will not let even a few people know
        Of any good qualities I might possess.

(165)   In short, may the harm I have caused others
        For the sake of myself
        Return and ripen upon me
        For the sake of others.

(166) I should not be domineering
       Or act in self-righteous ways.
       Rather, I should be like a newly-wed
       Who is bashful, timid and restrained.

(167) In this way, selfish mind, you should avoid
           non-virtue.
       If you do not observe this discipline,
       I will bring you under control
       Through the power of mindfulness and alertness.

(168) However, if you choose not to act
       In the way that you have been advised,
       Since you are the source of all my misfortune
       I will completely annihilate you.

(169) The time when you could govern me
       Has been consigned to the past.
       Now that I see you to be the source of all my
           problems,
       I will eradicate you wherever you appear.

(170) Now I will immediately cast aside
       All thoughts to work for my own sake.
       O self-cherishing mind, I have sold you to others;
       So stop complaining and get on with helping them!

(171) If, out of non-conscientiousness,
       I were not to give you to others,
       You would certainly deliver me
       To the guardians of hell!

(172)   You have done this to me often enough in the past
And, as a result, I have suffered for a very long
     time;
But now that I have brought to mind all my
     grudges towards you,
I am determined to destroy you, selfish mind.

(173)   Thus, if I want happiness,
I should not be happy with the self-cherishing
     mind;
And if I want protection,
I should always protect others.

(174)   To whatever extent I seek
To fulfil the desires of the body,
To that extent I shall experience
A state of dissatisfaction.

(175)   The desires of the self-cherishing mind
Cannot be satisfied
Even by all the wealth in the world –
So how can we hope to fulfil all its wishes?

(176)   When our desires are not fulfilled,
We develop delusions and a dissatisfied mind;
But whoever becomes free from such distracting
     concerns
Will never know dissatisfaction.

(177)   Therefore, I will never allow
The desires of the body to increase.
A person who has no attachment to attractive
     objects
Will find contentment – the best of all possessions.

(178) My body is a frightening, impure form
       That cannot move without depending upon mind
       And that eventually will completely disintegrate;
       So why do I grasp at it as 'I'?

(179) Whether it lives or dies,
       What use is it to me to grasp at this machine?
       It is no different from grasping at a clod of earth;
       So why do I not give up the pride of grasping 'my
           body'?

(180) As a result of attending to the body's desires,
       I have experienced much suffering without real
           meaning.
       What is the point of generating anger or attachment
       For the sake of something that is like a piece of
           wood?

(181) Whether I care for it in the way that I do,
       Or allow it to be harmed by others,
       The body itself develops neither attachment nor
           anger;
       So why do I feel so attached to it?

(182) Since the body itself does not know
       Anger when it is insulted
       Or attachment when it is praised,
       Why do I go to so much trouble for its sake?

(183) *'But I want to cherish this body*
       Because it is very beneficial to me.'
       Then why not cherish all living beings,
       For they are very beneficial to us?

(184)   Therefore, without any attachment,
        I will give up my body for the benefit of all;
        But, although it might have many faults,
        I will look after it while I am working for others.

(185)   I will put a stop to all childish behaviour
        And follow in the steps of the wise Bodhisattvas.
        Recalling the instructions on conscientiousness,
        I will turn away from sleep, mental dullness and the
            like.

(186)   Just like the compassionate Sons and Daughters of
            the Conqueror Buddha,
        I will patiently apply myself to whatever needs to be
            done.
        If I do not apply constant effort throughout the day
            and the night,
        When will my misery ever come to an end?

(187)   Therefore, to dispel both obstructions,
        I will withdraw my mind from all distracting
            conceptions
        And place it in constant meditative equipoise
        On the perfect object of meditation, the correct view
            of emptiness.

This concludes the eighth chapter of *Guide to the Bodhisattva's Way of Life*, entitled 'Relying upon Mental Stabilization'.

Chapter 9:

The Perfection of Wisdom

Buddha taught all the method practices explained above
To enable us to complete the training in wisdom realizing
  emptiness.
Therefore, those who wish to liberate themselves and
  others from suffering
Should strive to develop this wisdom.

The Perfection of Wisdom

(1)   Buddha taught all the method practices explained above
To enable us to complete the training in wisdom realizing emptiness.
Therefore, those who wish to liberate themselves and others from suffering
Should strive to develop this wisdom.

(2)   The two truths are explained as conventional truths and ultimate truths.
Ultimate truth, emptiness, is a non-affirming negative phenomenon
That cannot be realized directly by a mind that has dualistic appearance,
For such minds are conventional, and thus mistaken awareness.

(3)   Of those who assert the two truths, two types of
          person can be distinguished:
      Madhyamika-Prasangika Yogis and proponents of
          things.
      The views held by the proponents of things, who
          assert that things are truly existent,
      Are refuted by the logical reasonings of the
          Prasangika Yogis.

(4)   Moreover, among the Prasangika Yogis, there are
          different levels of insight –
      Those with greater understanding surpassing those
          with lesser understanding.
      All establish their view through valid analytical
          reasons.
      Giving and so forth are practised without
          investigation for the sake of achieving resultant
          Buddhahood.

(5)   When you proponents of things see things,
      You do not recognize their illusion-like character
      But assert them to be inherently existent.
      This is where we Madhyamika-Prasangikas disagree
          with you.

(6)   Forms that we see directly are just mere appearance
          to mind.
      They exist falsely because the way they appear
      Does not correspond to the way they exist,
      Just as a human body is conventionally accepted as
          clean when in reality it is impure.

(7)   Buddha taught the impermanence of things
        To lead people gradually to a realization of
            emptiness –
        The lack of inherent existence of things.
        *'Then it is incorrect to say that things exist even
            conventionally.'*

(8)   No, there is no fault, because things exist by
            conventional valid cognizers.
        From the point of view of worldly people, seeing
            things is seeing reality;
        But worldly people never actually see reality
        Because the real nature of things is their emptiness.

(9)   Just as you receive merits you consider to be truly
            existent from making offerings to a Buddha you
            consider to be truly existent,
        So we receive illusion-like merits from making
            offerings to an illusion-like Buddha.
        *'If, as you say, living beings lack true existence and are
            like illusions,
        How can they take rebirth after they die?'*

(10)   Provided all the necessary conditions are assembled,
        Even an illusion will come into being.
        Why, simply by virtue of their longer duration,
        Should living beings be any more true?

(11)   Killing an illusion incurs no actual karma of killing
        Because an illusion has no mind,
        But benefiting or harming an illusion-like person
            who has an illusion-like mind
        Gives rise to merit and negativity respectively.

155

(12) Because the mantras and so forth that cause an
       illusion cannot produce mind,
An illusion does not develop a mind.
Different types of cause
Give rise to different types of illusion.

(13) There does not exist a single cause that is capable of
Giving rise to a variety of different results.
'If, as you say, nirvana is not truly existent,
But samsara exists conventionally,

(14) *'Then Buddha must be in samsara because nirvana does*
      not exist;
So what is the point of practising the Bodhisattva's way
      of life?'
Even an illusion does not cease if the continuum of
      its causes is not cut,
But once the continuum of samsara's causes,
      delusions, is severed,

(15) Samsara will not occur, even conventionally.
Since Buddhas have done this, they have attained
      nirvana.
'The illusion-like forms that you assert do not exist,
Because you assert that illusion-like awareness lacks
      true existence.'

(16) Since for you Chittamatrins such illusion-like forms
      do not exist,
How do forms exist?
'Although forms do not exist as external objects, they do
      exist in another way –
A form is an aspect, the nature of the mind to which it
      appears.'

(17) You Chittamatrins assert that mind itself appears in
          the aspect of form.
      If this is so, how does the mind arise?
      Buddha, the Protector of the World, has said
      That the mind cannot behold itself.

(18) For example, just as the blade of a sword cannot
          cut itself,
      So a mind cannot behold itself.
      *'On the contrary, just as a lamp can illuminate both itself
          and the objects around it,*
      So the mind can behold both itself and other phenomena.'

(19) If a lamp illuminates itself, then darkness obscures
          itself,
      And it follows that no one can see darkness because
          it is obscured!
      *'When clear crystal turns blue, it does so in dependence
          upon something else;*
      *But lapis lazuli is by nature blue – it does not depend
          upon anything else to appear blue.*

(20) *'Similarly, some awarenesses are related to objects other
          than themselves,*
      Whereas others, such as self-cognizers, are not.'
      The blueness of lapis lazuli does not exist without
          depending upon anything else –
      It does not create its own nature!

(21) *'Even though a lamp does not illuminate itself, it is the nature of illumination.'*
Then you should say that mind does not know itself
But is the nature of conscious illumination.
However, you cannot say that it is known by a mind that is substantially different from itself.

(22) According to you, if there is no truly existent awareness that knows mind,
Then mind does not exist;
In which case it makes no more sense to discuss whether the mind illuminates itself or not
Than it does to discuss the looks of the daughter of a childless person.

(23) *'If self-cognizers do not exist,*
How do we remember subjective consciousness?'
When we remember the object experienced, we remember the consciousness related to it,
Just as we would recall being poisoned by an animal bite when we experienced the pain that subsequently occurred.

(24) *'If people who have attained states such as tranquil abiding can see the minds of others far away,*
Surely one can see one's own mind, which is very close.'
People who apply magical eye lotion can see treasure vases deep beneath the ground,
But they cannot see the lotion!

(25) We have no intention of refuting the existence of
Eye awareness, ear awareness or any other
awareness.
What needs to be abandoned is the awareness that
grasps at truly existent forms and so forth,
Which is the fundamental cause of all suffering.

(26) *'Illusion-like forms are not other than the mind,*
But neither can they be considered to be one with the
mind.'
If they are true, why say they are not other than the
mind?
And if they are not other than the mind, why say
they are true?

(27) Just as illusion-like forms lack any true existence,
So it is with the mind that beholds them.
'Samsara, like all imputed objects, must have something
substantial as its basis;
Otherwise, it would be completely empty, just like space.'

(28) If imputed phenomena, such as samsara, had truly
existent bases,
How could you ever become bound in samsara and
how could you ever escape from it?
According to you, mind cannot be an apprehender
related to something it apprehends;
Rather, it must be an isolated cognition of itself.

(29)   If the mind exists inherently, or independently,
Then it is already free from all defilements,
And it follows that all living beings are already
    enlightened!
So what is the point of teaching that everything is
    just the nature of mind?

(30)   *'How does realizing that all phenomena are like illusions
Eliminate delusions?
After all, a magician who creates an illusion of a woman
Can still develop attachment for that illusory woman.'*

(31)   This is because the magician has not abandoned
The deluded tendency to grasp at true existence.
Thus, when he beholds the illusory woman,
His tendency to perceive her emptiness is very weak.

(32)   By developing acquaintance with the view of
    emptiness,
We shall eventually abandon grasping at true
    existence;
And especially by meditating on the emptiness of
    emptiness,
We shall come to abandon grasping at emptiness
    itself as being truly existent.

(33)   When it is said that 'No thing exists',
This means that truly existent things do not exist;
So how could a mind grasping at the true existence
    of that emptiness remain
When the basis for such a misconception – grasping
    at true existence – has been removed?

(34)   Eventually, when the true existence of things and
        the true existence of emptiness
       No longer appear to the mind,
       Since there is no other aspect of true existence,
       The mind will abide in the resultant pacified state
        in which all conceptuality has ceased.

(35)   Just as wishfulfilling jewels and wish-granting trees
        fulfil the hopes of humans and gods
       Even though they have no conceptual mind,
       So, through the force of the prayers they previously
        made and the merit accumulated by fortunate
        beings,
       Buddhas manifest physical forms in this world.

(36)   For example, although the Brahmin who consecrated
       The substance in the reliquary known as the
        'Garuda'
       Has long since passed away,
       The reliquary continues to alleviate poisons and so
        forth.

(37)   In a similar fashion, a Bodhisattva, while training
        on the path,
       Creates the 'reliquary' of a Buddha through his
        collections of merit and wisdom;
       And, although he eventually passes beyond sorrow,
       He continues to bestow both temporary and
        ultimate benefits upon all living beings.

(38)   *'But if Buddha has no conceptual mind,*
       How can there be meritorious results from making
           offerings to him?'
       It is said in the scriptures that the results will be
           the same
       Whether the Buddha to whom we make offerings
           is living or has passed away.

(39)   Moreover, the scriptures say that the results we
           receive depend upon our degree of faith,
       Whether we think Buddha is conventionally or
           ultimately existent when we make the offerings.
       Just as you receive merits from making offerings to
           a Buddha you consider to be truly existent,
       So do we receive merits from making offerings to
           an illusion-like Buddha.

(40)   *'Since we can attain liberation by gaining a direct*
           realization of the four noble truths,
       What is the point of striving to realize emptiness, lack of
           true existence?'
       It is necessary because the scriptures explain
           that without the path of wisdom realizing this
           emptiness,
       It is impossible to attain even the small
           enlightenment of self-liberation.

(41-4) *'Because we do not believe in the Mahayana, your quoting
from Mahayana scriptures is pointless.'*
We both believe that the Hinayana scriptures are
valid;
So you should apply your reasons for believing the
Hinayana equally to the Mahayana.
Thus, we understand that both are the holy Dharma
taught by Buddha himself.

Because they do not understand its profundity,
The Vaibhashika schools deny the Mahayana;
And because they do not believe in nirvana,
Some non-Buddhist schools deny the Hinayana.

Buddha's purpose in teaching both the Mahayana
and the Hinayana
Was to lead living beings to permanent liberation
from the cycle of suffering.
Focusing on this ultimate aim, practitioners of both
the Mahayana and the Hinayana
Emphasize the three higher trainings of moral
discipline, concentration and wisdom.

(45) Buddha gave his teachings as medicine to cure the
disease of the delusions, the cause of all suffering.
Some of his teachings are simple and others are very
profound.
If you do not understand his higher, more profound
teachings,
You should not simply conclude that they were not
taught by Buddha.

(46)   The great Master Kashyapa gathered many of
          Buddha's teachings,
       Principally the *Perfection of Wisdom Sutras*, Buddha's
          Mahayana teachings.
       However, the Vaibhashika schools do not
          understand the profound meaning of the
          Perfection of Wisdom Sutras;
       Thus, they conclude that these Sutras are not
          Buddha's teachings.

(47)   The principal holders of Buddhadharma were said
          to be those who have attained nirvana, the Arhats;
       But the Arhats that you proponents of things assert
       Cannot be real Arhats because, according to your
          view,
       Their minds still grasp at truly existent things.

(48)   *'They attained nirvana, or liberation, and became Arhats*
          because they abandoned their delusions.'
       You seem to think that, simply by abandoning
          manifest delusions, one immediately becomes an
          Arhat;
       But it is clear that even though a person might have
          temporarily abandoned manifest delusions,
       Nevertheless, he or she still bears the karmic
          potentials to be reborn in samsara.

(49)   *'The abandonment that Arhats achieve is not temporary.*
         They definitely do not take rebirth in samsara again
       Because they completely abandon craving, the principal
         cause of such rebirth.'
       But just as you say that they have non-deluded
         confusion,
       Why not also say that they have non-deluded
         craving?

(50)   These so-called Arhats have pleasant feelings
       That they apprehend to be truly existent.
       Because of feeling, craving develops –
       So they must be subject to the craving.

(51)   Although for a person who has not realized
         emptiness – the lack of truly existent things –
       Manifest delusions might be temporarily abandoned,
         eventually they will manifest again,
       Just as feelings and discriminations return when
         the concentration on the absorption without
         discrimination ends.
       Therefore, you must strive to realize emptiness to
         attain even solitary liberation.

(52)   The result of a Bodhisattva's meditation on
         emptiness
       Is the ability to remain in the abodes of samsara
       Out of compassion for those who suffer due to
         confusion,
       And free from the extremes of attachment and fear.

(53) Since the realization of emptiness is the antidote that
   removes the darkness
  Of the delusion-obstructions and the obstructions to
   knowing,
  Why do those who wish to attain enlightenment
  Not meditate on emptiness right away?

(54) Thus, it is quite inappropriate to cast aspersions
  On those who hold the view of emptiness;
  Rather, you should meditate without any doubt
  On emptiness, lack of true existence.

(55) By all means, be afraid of something
  That is the principal cause of samsaric suffering;
  But, since meditation on emptiness eliminates this
   suffering,
  Why should you be afraid of emptiness?

(56) If there were a truly existent I,
  It would make sense to be afraid of certain things;
  But, since there is no truly existent I,
  Who is there to be afraid?

(57) The teeth, hair or nails are not the I,
  Nor are the bones or blood.
  The mucus and phlegm are not the I,
  Nor are the lymph or pus.

(58) The body's fat or sweat are not the I,
  Nor are the lungs or liver.
  None of the other inner organs is the I,
  Nor are the excrement or urine.

(59)   The flesh or skin are not the I,
         Nor are the body's warmth or winds.
         The space element of the body is not the I,
         Nor are any of the six consciousnesses.

(60)   If, as the Samkhya school asserts, a permanent
              consciousness is the I,
         Then the consciousness that enjoys sound is also
              permanent;
         But how can it continue to enjoy sound
         When the object, sound, is no longer present?

(61)   If it can be a subjective consciousness even though
              its object does not exist,
         Then it follows that even a piece of wood can be a
              subjective consciousness.
         Nothing can be established as a consciousness
         If there is no object of which to be conscious.

(62)   'When no sound is present, the consciousness enjoys other
              objects such as visual forms.'
         But if it is permanent, why does it not continue to
              apprehend sound?
         'Because there is no sound in the vicinity at that time.'
         Well, if there is no object, sound, then there is no
              subjective apprehender of sound!

(63)   Moreover, how can an awareness whose nature it is
          to apprehend sound
       Also be an awareness whose nature it is to
          apprehend visual forms?
       *'It is like one person who can be considered to be both a
          father and a son.'*
       But this is mere imputation; he is not by nature both.

(64)   The analogy of father and son does not work for you
          Samkhyas.
       According to you, the independent creator of all
          manifests all forms.
       Thus, father and son must be one nature, as must
          an apprehender of sound and an apprehender of
          visual forms –
       But such things are not seen by a valid mind.

(65)   *'It is like an actor changing roles and being seen in
          different aspects.'*
       Well, if the I changes in this way, it cannot be
          permanent!
       *'Although the aspects change, its nature remains one and
          the same.'*
       But you cannot establish an unchangeable nature of
          the I, because you deny the ultimate nature of I,
          the lack of a truly existent I.

(66)   *'The different aspects are not true, only their nature is.'*
         If the aspects are not true, why say their nature is
              true?
         *'Their nature is true and the same in that they are both
              merely conscious apprehenders.'*
         Well then, all living beings must be one and the same
              because they are all conscious apprehenders.

(67)   Moreover, it follows that animate and inanimate
              phenomena must be one and the same,
         As creations of the general principle, the
              independent creator of all.
         If all the particular aspects are false,
         How can their basis, their nature, be true?

(68)   The material I asserted by materialists also cannot be
              the I,
         Because it is devoid of mind, just like a jug.
         *'But it has a relationship with mind and so it can know
              objects.'*
         When the self, or I, comes to know something, the
              former self that did not know ceases;

(69)   But if, as you say, the self is permanent and
              unchanging,
         How can it form a relationship with mind and
              become a knower?
         Saying that the self is devoid of mind and unable to
              function
         Is like saying that space is the self, or I!

(70)   *'If the self were not permanent but perished in the next
            moment,*

        *There would be no relationship between actions and their
            effects*

        *Because, if the self perished the moment it committed an
            action,*

        Who would there be to experience its fruits?'

(71)   There is no point in our arguing about this,
        Because we both assert that the continuum of a
            person who commits an action
        Is not different from the continuum of the person
            who experiences its effect;
        But at the time of experiencing the effect, the person
            who committed the causal action no longer exists;

(72)   And at the time of committing the causal action,
        It is impossible to see the person experiencing the
            effects.
        Both the committer of the action and the experiencer
            of its effects
        Are merely imputed upon a single continuum of a
            collection of aggregates.

(73)   Neither the mind of the past nor the mind of the
            future is the self,
        Because the former has ceased and the latter has yet
            to be produced.
        *'But surely the mind arising in the present moment is the
            self.'*
        If it were, then the self would not exist in the next
            moment!

170

(74) If you peel away the layers of the trunk of a plantain
tree,
You will never discover anything substantial.
In the same way, if you conduct a detailed analysis,
You will never be able to find a self, or I.

(75) *'If living beings have no true existence,*
For whom can we develop compassion?'
We promise to achieve the goal of Buddhahood
For the sake of those whom ignorance imputes as
truly existent.

(76) *'If living beings do not truly exist, who will gain the*
results of meditating on compassion?'
It is true that the cause, meditation on compassion,
and the result, Buddhahood, do not truly exist;
but they do exist nominally.
Thus, so that the suffering of all living beings may
be completely pacified,
We should not reject the nominally existent
compassion which leads to that result.

(77) It is suffering and its causes that need to be
abandoned,
And it is the ignorance of self-grasping that causes
delusions and suffering to increase.
'But there is no way to abandon self-grasping so that it
will never recur.'
On the contrary, meditation on selflessness,
or emptiness, is the supreme method for
accomplishing this.

(78)   Neither the feet nor the calves are the body,
       Nor are the thighs or the loins.
       Neither the front nor the back of the abdomen is
           the body,
       Nor are the chest or the shoulders.

(79)   Neither the sides nor the hands are the body,
       Nor are the arms or the armpits.
       None of the inner organs is the body,
       Nor is the head or the neck.
       So where is the body to be found?

(80)   If you say that the body is distributed
       Among all its different parts,
       Although we can say that the parts exist in the
           parts,
       Where does a separate possessor of these parts
           abide?

(81)   And if you say that the entire body exists
       Within each part, such as the hand,
       It follows that there are as many bodies
       As there are different parts!

(82)   If a truly existent body cannot be found either inside
           or outside the body,
       How can there be a truly existent body among the
           parts such as the hands?
       And since there is no body separate from its parts,
       How can there be a truly existent body at all?

(83)   Therefore, there is no body,
But, because of ignorance, we see a body within the
    hands and so forth,
Just like a mind mistakenly apprehending a person
When observing the shape of a pile of stones at dusk.

(84)   For as long as the causes of mistaking the stones for
    a person are present,
There will be a mistaken apprehension of the body
    of a person.
Likewise, for as long as the hands and so forth are
    grasped as truly existent,
There will be an apprehension of a truly existent
    body.

(85)   Just as the body lacks true existence, so do its parts
    such as the hands;
For they too are merely imputed upon the collection
    of their parts, the fingers and so forth.
The fingers, in turn, are merely imputed upon the
    collection of their parts, such as the joints;
And, when the joints are separated into their parts,
    they too are found to lack true existence.

(86)   The parts of the joints are merely imputed upon a
    collection of atoms,
And they, in turn, are merely imputed upon their
    directional parts.
Since the directional parts, too, can be further
    divided,
Atoms lack true existence and are empty, like space.

(87)   Therefore, what intelligent person
Would develop attachment for this dream-like form?
And since there is no truly existent body,
Who is truly existent male and who is truly existent
    female?

(88)   If painful feelings are truly existent, they can never
    be changed,
And it follows that living beings never experience
    pleasant feelings.
And if pleasant feelings are truly existent,
Why do delicious tastes not bring joy to one who is
    grieving?

(89)   *'Such a person does develop pleasant feelings, but he or*
    she does not experience them
Because they are suppressed by the strength of the painful
    feelings.'
How can there possibly be a feeling
That is not experienced?

(90)   *'When a strong pleasant feeling occurs, there is still a*
    subtle painful feeling.
The gross feeling of pain is dispelled, and the subtle pain
    that remains
Becomes the nature of a subtle pleasant feeling.'
Well then, that subtle feeling is a pleasant feeling, not
    a painful one!

(91)   *'So what you are saying is that painful feelings do not*
        occur at that time
    Because the delicious taste is a cause of their opposite –
        pleasant feelings.'
    Whether it is a cause of pleasant or painful feelings
        depends merely upon conceptual imputation;
    Thus, feelings are established as having no inherent
        existence.

(92)   The antidote that abandons grasping at truly existent
        feelings
    Is meditation on and analysis of lack of true
        existence.
    The superior seeing that arises from analysis of this
        emptiness, conjoined with tranquil abiding,
    Is the food that nourishes the Yogi's realizations.

(93)   If there is space between the partless particles of a
        sense power and those of its object,
    How can you maintain that they have met?
    But if there is no space between them, they must mix
        and become completely one;
    In which case, what is it that meets with what?

(94)   But one partless particle could never penetrate
        another
    Because they would both be equal in size without
        any empty space inside.
    Without penetrating, they could not mix;
    And without mixing, they could not meet.

(95)   To say that two partless things can meet
         Is completely illogical.
         If it were possible, you would be able to detect it;
         So please show me an example!

(96)   There can be no truly existent meeting between
             consciousness and form
         Because consciousness has no material qualities.
         Moreover, as we explained previously, there is no
             truly existent collection;
         So there is no truly existent collection of material
             particles with which to meet.

(97)   Thus, if contact is not truly existent,
         The feeling that arises from it must also lack true
             existence.
         So why exhaust yourself pursuing pleasant feelings?
         And, if there are no truly existent painful feelings,
             who can be harmed by what?

(98)   If there are no truly existent feelings,
         There is no truly existent person to experience them.
         Seeing this to be the case,
         Why do we not abandon our craving?

(99)   All objects of consciousness that give rise to feelings
             – from visual forms to tactile objects –
         Are like dreams and illusions, utterly devoid of true
             existence.
         If the mind experiencing feelings is truly existent,
         It cannot experience any feelings that arise
             simultaneously with it.

(100)   Moreover, even if you assert that it can remember
feelings that have passed, it cannot experience
them;

And it cannot experience feelings that have yet to
arise because they do not exist.

So, feelings cannot experience themselves,

And no truly existent other consciousness can
experience them either.

(101)   Thus, since the person who experiences feelings
does not truly exist

And feelings themselves do not truly exist,

How can this selfless collection of aggregates

Be harmed or benefited by painful or pleasant
feelings?

(102)   Mental consciousness cannot be found in the six
powers,

In the six objects of consciousnesses, such as forms,
or in the collection of the two.

It cannot be found either inside or outside of the
body,

Nor can it be found anywhere else.

(103)   Mental consciousness is neither the body nor
inherently other than the body.

It is not mixed with the body, nor is it entirely
separate from it.

It is not the slightest bit truly existent.

This lack of true existence, the emptiness of the
mind, is called the 'natural state of nirvana'.

(104) If a sense awareness exists prior to its object,
What is it aware of?
If it arises simultaneously with its object,
In dependence upon what object does it arise?

(105) And if a sense awareness is truly existent,
How can it arise subsequently in dependence upon
an object condition?
In this way, we can understand
That all six consciousnesses lack true existence.

(106) *'Well then, it follows that phenomena cannot exist even
conventionally,*
*In which case your presentation of the two truths is
invalid.*
*Moreover, if conventional truths are merely imputed by
mistaken minds,*
*How can living beings pass beyond sorrow even
nominally?'*

(107) According to our system, to exist conventionally
Does not mean to be imputed by a mind grasping at
true existence.
A conventional truth, such as body, is imputed by a
valid conceptual mind having perceived a valid
basis of imputation.
Without such imputation by a valid mind, there
would be no conventional truths.

(108)   The imputing mind and the object imputed
        Are established in mutual dependence upon each
            other.
        Each distinct phenomenon is posited by an
            analytical mind
        According to what is validly known in the world.

(109)   *'When an analytical mind realizes an object to be
            non-truly existent,*
        *Another analytical mind must analyze that mind to
            realize that it too is non-truly existent.*
        *That analytical mind, in turn, must be analyzed by
            another,*
        And so the process is endless, which is absurd.'

(110)   When a valid mind directly realizes the lack of true
            existence of all phenomena,
        The true existence of that mind is implicitly negated
            at the same time.
        This non-true existence of both subject and object
        Is also called the 'natural state of nirvana'.

(111)   Despite your attempts, you Chittamatrins are unable
            to establish
        The true existence of the apprehending mind and
            the object apprehended.
        *'On the contrary, forms, for example, are truly existent
            because consciousness apprehends them to be so.'*
        How can you establish anything with a
            consciousness that is truly existent?

(112) *'We can establish that consciousness is truly existent
    because the objects it apprehends are truly existent.'*
    If you say this, on what basis is the true existence of
        these objects established,
    Given that they and the consciousness that
        apprehends them are mutually dependent?
    Surely this demonstrates that both consciousness
        and its object lack true existence.

(113) For example, if a man has no child, he cannot be a
        father;
    And if there is no father, how can there be a child?
    Since without a child, there is no father, they are
        mutually dependent and therefore neither is truly
        existent.
    It is likewise with consciousness and its object.

(114) *'From the fact that a truly existent sprout arises from a
    seed,*
    We can understand the true existence of the seed.
    *So why, from the fact that a truly existent consciousness
        arises from an object,*
    *Can we not understand that the object too is truly
        existent?'*

(115) It is true that the existence of a seed can be inferred
        from the existence of its sprout
    By a consciousness that is substantially distinct from
        that sprout;
    But what consciousness can cognize a truly existent
        consciousness
    That, according to you, indicates the true existence of
        its object?

(116) Even worldly people can see clearly
That most things arise from causes.
The different types of coloured lotus, for example,
Arise from a variety of different causes.

(117) *'And what gave rise to that variety of causes?'*
A previous variety of causes.
*'But how does a distinct cause give rise to a distinct
effect?'*
Each effect is produced from a specific potentiality
in its preceding cause.

(118) If you Samkhyas want to say that Ishvara is the
creator of all things,
Then please explain who or what Ishvara is.
'He is basically the nature of the four great elements.'
Then why go to the trouble of giving them the
name 'Ishvara'?

(119) Since the elements such as earth are multiple
substances,
Impermanent, unmoved by mind, non-divine
And something trodden upon and unclean,
They cannot possibly be Ishvara.

(120) Space is not Ishvara because it cannot produce
anything,
And a permanent self cannot be Ishvara because
this has already been refuted.
'Although he is the creator, Ishvara is unknowable.'
What is the point of talking about something that
cannot be known?

(121)   Precisely what is it that Ishvara is supposed to create?

'He creates the world, living beings, and his own subsequent continuum.'

But if this is so, how did such an independent creator himself develop?

Moreover, consciousness is produced from its previous continuum,

(122)   And, since beginningless time, happiness and suffering have been created by karma, or actions.

So, tell us, what does Ishvara create?

If the cause has no beginning,

The effect must also have no beginning.

(123)   So why, if their production does not depend upon other conditions,

Are effects such as happiness and suffering not constantly produced without interruption?

And if, as you say, there is nothing other than phenomena created by Ishvara,

Upon what conditions does Ishvara depend when he creates an effect?

(124)   If a collection of causes and conditions produces an effect,

That effect is not produced by Ishvara.

If the causes and conditions are assembled, even Ishvara does not have the power to prevent the effect being produced;

And, if they are not assembled, he cannot possibly produce that effect.

(125) If effects such as suffering are produced without
    Ishvara's wishing for them,
It follows that they are produced through the power
    of something other than him.
You say that all effects are produced according to
    Ishvara's wishes,
But those wishes have no power to produce all
    things, so how can Ishvara be the creator of
    everything?

(126) The assertion that the world and living beings are
    produced from permanent partless particles
Has already been refuted.
You Samkhyas assert that the creator is
The permanent general principle.

(127) You describe this general principle as a balanced
    state
Of three qualities: lightness, activity and darkness,
Which should be understood as the feelings of
    indifference, pleasure and pain.
Unbalanced states of these, you say, are the
    manifestations that constitute the world.

(128) If the general principle, the independent creator of
    all, has a threefold nature,
It is neither singular nor plural, and therefore does
    not exist.
Similarly, the individual qualities cannot exist
Because you say that each of them is a composite of
    the three qualities.

(129)   If the three qualities do not exist, the general
              principle does not exist,
         In which case it is impossible to establish its
              manifestations such as visual forms and sounds.
         And it is simply impossible for mindless things,
              such as clothing,
         To have the same nature as feelings, such as
              happiness.

(130)   *'All things truly exist in the nature of their causes.'*
         But we have already thoroughly refuted the
              possibility of truly existent things.
         According to you, clothing and the like arise from
              the general principle, which is a balanced state of
              pleasure and so forth;
         But this cannot be the case, because we have refuted
              the existence of such a general principle.

(131)   In fact, feelings such as pleasure arise from things
              such as wearing clothing;
         And when these causes are lacking, their effects –
              pleasure and so forth – do not occur.
         If the general principle were permanent, its nature of
              pleasure, for example, would also be permanent;
         But this has never been seen by a valid cognizer.

(132)   If pleasure were permanent, it would always be
              manifest;
         So why is it not experienced when pain is manifest?
         *'At those times, the gross feeling of pleasure becomes
              subtle.'*
         How can something that is permanent change from
              gross to subtle?

184

(133) Something that abandons a gross state and becomes
         subtle
       Is at one time gross and at another time subtle, and
         therefore impermanent.
       In the same way, you should assert
       That all functioning things are impermanent.

(134) If gross pleasure is not different from pleasure itself,
       Then clearly pleasure, and therefore the general
         principle, are impermanent.
       You assert that a manifest phenomenon does not
         exist at the time of its cause
       And thus that a product does not exist at the time of
         its cause.

(135) Although you do not want to assert that a manifest
         phenomenon that did not previously exist is
         produced anew,
       In reality this is what you are saying.
       If the effect exists as the same nature as its cause,
       Then eating food is the same as eating the excrement
         it produces!

(136) So instead of spending your money on clothes of
         woven cotton,
       You might as well purchase cotton seeds to wear!
       *'Worldly people do not see the effect at the time of the
         cause because of their confusion.'*
       Well, what about your teacher, Kapila? He must
         know because you say he is omniscient;

185

(137)   And since you teach his view to worldly people,
        Why can they not see the effect at the time of the
            cause?
        *'Because worldly people do not see things with valid
            cognizers.'*
        Then the manifest phenomena that they see clearly
            must also not be true!

(138)   *'According to you Madhyamikas, valid cognizers are not
            truly existent, and so they must be false,*
        *In which case the objects established by them must also be
            false.*
        If this is so, then the emptiness you assert is false,
        And meditating on it serves no purpose.'

(139)   Without first correctly identifying the object to be
            negated, true existence,
        You cannot apprehend its negation, or non-existence,
            emptiness.
        The negation of true existence, emptiness,
        Clearly has no true existence itself.

(140)   For example, if a mother dreams her child has died,
        The thought that the child no longer exists
        Removes the thought of the child's existence,
        Even though neither thought is truly existent.

(141)   Through these various lines of reasoning,
        We have established that production does not occur
            without a cause,
        And that a result, such as a sprout, does not exist in
            any of its causes and conditions,
        Either individually or collectively.

186

(142)   Effects do not come from anywhere else when they
            are produced,
        They do not go anywhere when they perish, and
            they do not inherently abide.
        They appear to be truly existent only because of
            ignorance,
        But in fact they are like illusions.

(143)   Examine something produced from causes
        And compare it with an illusion conjured up by a
            magician.
        Where do they come from when they arise?
        Where do they go to when they perish?

(144)   We can see that effects arise from causes
        And that, without a cause, there cannot be an effect.
        Thus, things are artificial, like reflections.
        How can they possibly be truly existent?

(145)   If something is truly existent,
        What need is there for a cause to produce it?
        And if something is non-existent,
        Again, what need is there for a cause to produce it?

(146)   Even with a hundred million causes,
        A non-thing will never transform into a thing.
        If it remained a non-thing, how could it become
            a thing?
        From what state could it transform into a thing?

(147)   While it is not a thing, it cannot exist as a thing;
        So when could it ever become a thing?
        It would be unable to separate from being a non-thing
        Without first becoming a thing;

187

(148)   But without its being separated from the state of
             being a non-thing,
         It is impossible for the state of a thing to arise.
         Likewise, a functioning thing cannot become a
             permanent phenomenon
         Because, if it did, it would have two mutually
             exclusive natures.

(149)   Just as there is no truly existent production of
             things,
         So there is no truly existent cessation.
         Thus, living beings are not truly born,
         Nor do they truly cease.

(150)   Living beings are like objects in a dream
         For, when analyzed, they have no ultimate identity,
             just like a rainbow.
         Thus, in that they both lack true existence, there is
             no difference
         Between nirvana, the state beyond sorrow, and
             samsara, the state of sorrow.

(151)   With objects that are empty in this way,
         What is there to gain and what is there to lose?
         Who is there to praise me?
         And who is there to blame me?

(152)   With no truly existent benefit or harm,
         What is there to be happy or unhappy about?
         And, when their ultimate nature is sought,
         Where are those who seek a good reputation, and
             where is what they seek?

(153) When examined in this way,
       Who is living and who is it who will die?
       What is the future and what is the past?
       Who are our friends and who are our relatives?

(154) I beseech you who are just like me,
       Please know that all things are empty, like space.
       Consider that although all people wish for
            happiness,
       They swing between being troubled by suffering

(155) And being overjoyed by meaningless pleasure.
       Not finding happiness, they suffer; and in striving to
            fulfil their wishes
       They quarrel, fight and hurt each other with
            weapons.
       Thus, they consume their lives in the commission of
            non-virtue.

(156) From time to time, they take a fortunate rebirth
       And briefly enjoy some temporary happiness,
       But soon they die and fall into the lower realms,
       Where they experience unbearable suffering for a
            very long time.

(157) In samsara, there are many pitfalls that lead to
            suffering.
       Instead of finding the path of emptiness that leads to
            freedom,
       We are bound by its opposite, grasping at true
            existence.
       But if, while in samsara, we do not find the path of
            emptiness,

189

(158) We shall continue to experience an unending ocean
of suffering
That is so unbearable it is beyond analogy.
Even in fortunate rebirths, we shall have little ability
to practise virtue,
And our lives of freedom and endowment will
quickly pass.

(159) We are constantly striving to avoid sickness and
death,
Fend off hunger, find some rest, or just get to sleep.
We receive harm from inner and outer obstacles,
And waste our lives in meaningless company.

(160) Thus, our life passes swiftly without any meaning,
And we find it very hard to realize emptiness.
In such a state, where is there a method to reverse
The deluded wanderings of the mind, with which
we are so familiar?

(161) Furthermore, demonic forces are constantly striving
To cast us into the vast wasteland of the lower
realms.
There are many mistaken paths to mislead us,
And we find it difficult to resolve stultifying doubts.

(162) It will be very hard to find the freedom and
endowment of a human rebirth again.
Buddhas rarely appear in this world, and it is
difficult to find a qualified Mahayana Spiritual
Guide.

Without these, there is no way to stop the flood of
    delusions –
Alas, the suffering of living beings will continue
    without interruption!

(163) Oh, surely we must feel compassion for all these
    poor beings
Who are swept along in these vast rivers of suffering,
For, although they suffer in the extreme,
They do not recognize their suffering state.

(164) For example, some ascetics repeatedly wash in
    freezing water
And burn themselves with fire again and again;
And, although they experience great suffering,
They proudly maintain that they are happy!

(165) In the same way, those who live their lives
As if they were not going to be struck by sufferings
    such as ageing and death,
Will experience horrendous suffering at the hands
    of the Lord of Death
And then be cast into the unbearable torments of
    the lower realms.

(166) May I be able to extinguish the fires of suffering
That torment all these beings,
With a vast rain of happiness
Descending from the clouds of my merit;

(167)   And, through sincerely accumulating a collection of
        merit,
       While endowed with the wisdom realizing non-true
        existence,
       May I teach emptiness to all living beings
       Who suffer because of their self-grasping.

This concludes the ninth chapter of *Guide to the Bodhisattva's Way of Life*, entitled 'The Perfection of Wisdom'.

Chapter 10:

Dedication

By virtue of my merits,
May all beings everywhere,
Tormented by sufferings of body and mind,
Find physical comfort and mental joy.

CHAPTER 10

Dedication

(1)   Through the virtues I have created
By composing *Guide to the Bodhisattva's Way of Life*,
May all living beings without exception
Practise the Bodhisattva's deeds.

(2)   By virtue of my merits,
May all beings everywhere,
Tormented by sufferings of body and mind,
Find physical comfort and mental joy.

(3)   For as long as they remain in samsara,
May their temporary happiness never decline;
And may they all eventually experience
The everlasting joy of Buddhahood.

(4)   May all embodied creatures
Throughout the universe
Who are experiencing the pains of hell
Enjoy the bliss of Sukhavati Pure Land.

(5)   May those tormented by cold find warmth,
And may those tormented by heat be cooled
By a continuous rain of soothing waters
Flowing from the vast clouds of the Bodhisattvas'
    merit and wisdom.

(6)   May the forest of razor-sharp leaves
Become a delightful woodland glade,
And may the trees of splintered iron and piercing
    thorns
Transform into wishfulfilling trees.

(7)   May the regions of hell become joyful lands
Adorned with vast and fragrant lotus pools
Resounding with the enchanting calls
Of wild geese, ducks and swans.

(8)   May the heaps of burning coals become piles of
    various jewels,
May the red-hot iron ground become a soothing
    crystal floor,
And may the mountains of the crushing hells
Become celestial palaces of worship filled with
    Sugatas.

(9)   May the hail of lava, blazing stones and weapons
Henceforth become a rain of flowers,
And may all attacks with weapons
From now on become a playful exchange of flowers.

(10)   May those drowning in the fiery torrents of acid –
        Their flesh eaten away to reveal their lily-white
            bones –
        Attain the bodies of celestial beings
        And sport with consorts in gently flowing streams.

(11)   *'Why are the henchmen of the Lord of Death and the*
            unbearable buzzards and vultures so afraid?
        By whose noble power is the darkness of our suffering
            dispelled and joy bestowed upon us?'
        Looking above them, those in hell will behold the
            radiant form of Vajrapani, the Holder of the Vajra.
        Through the force of their new-found faith and joy,
            may they be freed from past evil and come to
            abide with him.

(12)   When they see the lava fires of hell extinguished by a
            rain of flowers moist with scented waters,
        And are immediately satiated with bliss,
        They will wonder by whose hand this was brought
            about
        And behold Pemapani, the Holder of the Lotus.

(13)   *'Friends, cast away your fears and quickly gather here,*
        For above us is the youthful Manjushri, whose radiant
            topknot dispels all fears.
        Endowed with great compassion and bodhichitta, he
            protects all living beings,
        And through his power dispels all suffering and bestows
            perfect joy.

(14)   *'Behold him in his enchanting palace resounding with*
            the songs of a thousand celestial beings,
         With hundreds of gods bowing before him, their tiaras
            touching his lotus feet,
         And a vast rain of flowers falling upon his gracious head,
            his eyes moist with compassion.'
         Thus, upon seeing Manjushri, may all beings in
            hell cry out with joy.

(15)   Likewise, when through my roots of virtue all
            beings in hell
         Feel the cool, sweet-smelling rain descending
            from miraculous clouds
         Created by Bodhisattvas such as Samantabhadra,
         May they experience perfect happiness.

(16)   May all animals be freed from the fears
         Of being preyed upon by one another,
         And may all hungry spirits be as happy
         As the inhabitants of the northern continent.

(17)   May they be satiated by a stream of milk
         Flowing from the compassionate hands
         Of Arya Avalokiteshvara
         And, by bathing in it, may they be constantly
            refreshed.

(18)   May the blind see forms,
         May the deaf hear sounds,
         And just as it was with Mayadevi, the mother of
            Buddha,
         May all pregnant women give birth without pain.

(19)   May the naked find clothing,
May the hungry find food,
And may the thirsty find pure water
And delicious drinks.

(20)   May the poor find wealth,
May those weak with sorrow find joy,
And may those whose fortunes have declined
Find replenishment and long-lasting good
      fortune.

(21)   May everyone who is sick
Be swiftly healed,
And may every disease that affects living beings
Be permanently eradicated.

(22)   May the frightened be released from their fears,
May those in captivity be freed,
May the powerless be endowed with power
And may people think only of benefiting one
      another.

(23)   May travellers on the road
Find happiness wherever they go,
And without any effort
Accomplish whatever they set out to do.

(24)   May those who sail by ship or boat
Obtain whatever they seek
And, returning safely to the shore,
Joyfully reunite with their friends and relatives.

(25) May those distressed because they have lost their
way
Meet with fellow travellers
And, without any fear of thieves or other dangers,
Proceed comfortably without fatigue.

(26) May those in dangerous and fearful places,
Children, the aged and the unprotected,
As well as the bewildered and the insane,
Be guarded by benevolent celestials.

(27) May all humans be freed from all the unfree states,
May they be endowed with faith, wisdom and
compassion,
And may they have the very best food, follow pure
conduct
And always be concerned for their future lives.

(28) May they have inexhaustible joy and copious
resources,
Just like the supreme treasury;
And may they enjoy freedom,
With no disputes, interferences or injury.

(29) May those who possess little splendour
Be endowed with majesty,
And may those whose bodies are worn through
asceticism
Attain magnificent and noble forms.

(30) May all beings everywhere
Take rebirth in a gender of their choice,
And may the lowly and downcast attain grandeur
Without ever displaying pride.

(31) By the power of the merit I have accumulated,
May all living beings without exception
Abandon all forms of evil
And always engage in virtue.

(32) May they never be separated from bodhichitta
And always follow the Bodhisattva's way of life.
May they be cared for by Buddhas and Spiritual
    Guides
And forsake all demonic activity.

(33) While in samsara, may they be reborn in
    fortunate realms
And enjoy inconceivably long lives,
Abiding always in contentment
Without ever hearing the word 'death'.

(34) May all places throughout the world
Become gardens of wishfulfilling trees,
Resounding with the sound of Dharma
Proclaimed by Buddhas and Bodhisattvas.

(35) May the whole ground
Become completely pure,
As level as the palm of a hand,
And as smooth as lapis lazuli.

(36) And in every land may there appear,
For the sake of all disciples,
Multitudes of Bodhisattvas
Possessed of excellent qualities.

(37) May all living beings uninterruptedly hear
      The sweet sound of Dharma
      Issuing forth from birds and trees,
      Beams of light and even space itself.

(38) May they always meet with Buddhas
      And their Sons and Daughters, the Bodhisattvas;
      And may the Spiritual Guides of the world
      Be venerated with clouds of offerings.

(39) May celestial beings bring timely rains,
      And may harvests always be plentiful.
      May governments rule in accordance with
          Dharma,
      And may the people of the world prosper.

(40) May all medicines be effective,
      May the recitation of mantras fulfil all wishes,
      And may all spirits and animals who have
          influence over us
      Be endowed with great compassion.

(41) May no one ever experience physical pain,
      Mental anguish or sickness.
      May they be free from all forms of unhappiness,
      And may no one ever be afraid or belittled.

(42) In all temples and Dharma centres,
      May recitation and meditation flourish forever.
      May the Sangha always be in harmony,
      And may their wish to benefit others be fulfilled.

(43) May Sangha who wish to practise purely
Find the right conditions to do so
And, abandoning all distractions,
Meditate with mental suppleness.

(44) May the ordained be materially provided for
And always be free from harm.
May no one who has taken ordination
Ever allow their moral discipline to degenerate.

(45) May all those who have broken their moral
discipline
Completely purify their downfalls.
May they attain a fortunate rebirth
And never allow their morality to decline again.

(46) May those who are learned in Dharma be respected
And receive material support.
May their minds be pure and peaceful,
And may their good qualities be proclaimed in all
directions.

(47) May they never experience the sufferings of the
lower realms
Or meet with hardships of body, speech or mind.
May they have forms superior to those of the gods
And quickly attain the state of a Buddha.

(48) May all living beings again and again
Make offerings to the Buddhas.
May they become endowed with the eternal bliss
Of a fully enlightened being.

(49)   May the Bodhisattvas fulfil the welfare of the world
       In the very manner they have intended,
       And may all living beings receive
       Everything the Buddhas have intended for them.

(50)   Likewise, may all Solitary Realizers and Hearers
       Attain the happiness of nirvana.

(51)   And until I attain the level of the Joyous One,
       Through the blessings of Manjushri,
       May I be concerned for all my future lives
       And always receive ordination.

(52)   May I always live humbly, sustained by simple food.
       Throughout all my lives, may I abide in solitude
       And always find ideal conditions
       For achieving my spiritual goals.

(53)   Whenever I wish to see a scripture
       Or compose even a single verse,
       May I behold without obstruction
       Protector Manjushri.

(54)   To fulfil the needs of all living beings
       Reaching to the ends of space,
       May my way of life always resemble
       That of Manjushri.

(55)   For as long as space exists
       And for as long as living beings remain in samsara,
       May I abide among them
       To dispel all their suffering.

(56)   May all the suffering of all living beings
       Ripen solely upon me;
       And by the power of the Bodhisattvas' virtue and
           aspirations
       May all beings experience happiness.

(57)   May the Buddhadharma, the sole medicine for all
           suffering
       And the source of all happiness,
       Be materially supported and honoured,
       And remain for a very long time.

(58)   I prostrate to Manjushri,
       Through whose kindness my virtuous intentions
           arise;
       And I prostrate to my Spiritual Guide,
       Through whose kindness my virtuous qualities
           increase.

This concludes the tenth chapter of *Guide to the Bodhisattva's
Way of Life*, entitled 'Dedication'.

This concludes *Guide to the Bodhisattva's Way of Life*, composed
by the Buddhist Master Shantideva.

Glossary

Most of these terms are explained in detail in Venerable Geshe Kelsang Gyatso Rinpoche's commentary, entitled Meaningful to Behold. *Where more detail can be found in Venerable Geshe Kelsang Gyatso Rinpoche's other books, this is indicated in the glossary entry.*

Absorption without discrimination A concentration of the fourth form realm that observes nothingness and that is attained by stopping gross feelings and gross discriminations. See *Ocean of Nectar*.

Aggregates In general, all functioning things are aggregates because they are an aggregation of their parts. In particular, a person of the desire realm or form realm has five aggregates: the aggregates of form, feeling, discrimination, compositional factors and consciousness. A being of the formless realm lacks the aggregate of form but has the other four. A person's form aggregate is his or her body. The remaining four aggregates are aspects of his mind. See *The New Heart of Wisdom*.

Anger A deluded mental factor that observes its contaminated object, exaggerates its bad qualities, considers it to be undesirable and wishes to harm it. See *How to Solve Our Human Problems*.

Arhat   Sanskrit for 'Foe Destroyer'. A practitioner who has abandoned all delusions and their seeds by training on the spiritual paths, and who will never again be reborn in samsara. In this context, the term 'Foe' refers to the delusions.

Arya   Sanskrit for 'Superior being'. Someone who has a direct, or non-conceptual, realization of emptiness. There are Hinayana Superiors and Mahayana Superiors.

Aspiring bodhichitta   A mind that aspires to attain enlightenment for the benefit of all living beings but that does not yet engage in the actual practices of the Bodhisattva's training. It is like someone intending to go somewhere but not yet setting out on the journey.

Attachment   A deluded mental factor that observes a contaminated object, regards it as a cause of happiness, and wishes for it.

Avalokiteshvara   'Chenrezig' in Tibetan. The embodiment of the compassion of all the Buddhas.

Basis of imputation   All phenomena are imputed upon their parts; therefore, any of the individual parts, or the entire collection of the parts, of any phenomenon is its basis of imputation. A phenomenon is imputed by mind in dependence upon its basis of imputation appearing to that mind. See *The New Heart of Wisdom*.

Beginningless time   According to the Buddhist world view, there is no beginning to mind, and so no beginning to time. Therefore, all living beings have taken countless previous rebirths.

Blessings   The transformation of our mind from a negative state to a positive state, from an unhappy state to a happy state, or from a state of weakness to a state of strength, through the inspiration of holy beings such as our Spiritual Guide, Buddhas and Bodhisattvas.

Bodhichitta Sanskrit for 'mind of enlightenment'. 'Bodhi' means 'enlightenment', and 'chitta' means 'mind'. There are two types of bodhichitta – conventional bodhichitta and ultimate bodhichitta. Generally speaking, the term 'bodhichitta' refers to conventional bodhichitta, which is a primary mind motivated by great compassion that spontaneously seeks enlightenment to benefit all living beings. There are two types of conventional bodhichitta – aspiring bodhichitta and engaging bodhichitta. Ultimate bodhichitta is a wisdom motivated by conventional bodhichitta that directly realizes emptiness, the ultimate nature of phenomena. See also *Aspiring bodhichitta* and *Engaging bodhichitta*.

Bodhisattva A person who has generated spontaneous bodhichitta but who has not yet become a Buddha.

Brahma A worldly god, who resides in the first form realm.

Buddha A being who has completely abandoned all delusions and their imprints. Every living being has the potential to become a Buddha.

Chakravatin king An extremely fortunate being who has accumulated a vast amount of merit and as a result has taken rebirth as a king with dominion over all the four continents as described in Buddhist cosmology, or, at the very least, over one of the four continents. At present there are no chakravatin kings in our world, and there is no one who has complete dominion over our continent, Jambudipa. See *Great Treasury of Merit*.

Chekhawa, Bodhisattva (1102-1176 CE) A great Kadampa Bodhisattva who composed the text *Training the Mind in Seven*

Points, a commentary to Bodhisattva Langri Tangpa's *Eight Verses of Training the Mind*. He spread the study and practice of training the mind throughout Tibet. See *Universal Compassion*.

Chittamatrin A proponent of Chittamatra tenets, the lower of the two schools of Mahayana tenets. 'Chittamatra' means 'mind only'. Chittamatrins are so-called because they assert that all phenomena are merely the nature of mind. See *Ocean of Nectar*.

Collection of merit A virtuous action motivated by bodhichitta that is a main cause of attaining the Form Body of a Buddha. Examples are: making offerings and prostrations to holy beings with bodhichitta motivation, and the practice of the perfections of giving, moral discipline and patience.

Collection of wisdom A virtuous mental action motivated by bodhichitta that is a main cause of attaining the Truth Body of a Buddha. Examples are: listening to, contemplating and meditating on emptiness with bodhichitta motivation.

Compassion A virtuous mind that wishes others to be free from suffering. See *The New Eight Steps to Happiness, Universal Compassion* and *Modern Buddhism*.

Concentration A mental factor that makes its primary mind remain on its object single-pointedly.

Conceptual mind A thought that apprehends its object through a generic, or mental, image. See *How to Understand the Mind*.

Confession Purification of negative karma by means of the four opponent powers. See *The Bodhisattva Vow*.

Conscientiousness A mental factor that, in dependence upon effort, cherishes what is virtuous and guards the mind from delusion and non-virtue. See *How to Understand the Mind*.

210

Contact A mental factor that functions to perceive its object as pleasant, unpleasant, or neutral. See *How to Understand the Mind*.

Contentment A happy mind that functions to prevent the problem of discontent.

Conventional truth Any phenomenon other than emptiness. Conventional truths are true with respect to the minds of ordinary beings, but in reality they are false. See *The New Heart of Wisdom*.

Dedication Dedication is by nature a virtuous mental factor; it is the virtuous intention that functions both to prevent accumulated virtue from degenerating and to cause its increase. See *Joyful Path of Good Fortune*.

Delusion A mental factor that arises from inappropriate attention and functions to make the mind unpeaceful and uncontrolled. There are three main delusions: ignorance, attachment and anger. From these arise all the other delusions, such as jealousy, pride and deluded doubt. See *How to Understand the Mind*.

Demi-god A being of the demi-god realm, the second highest of the six realms of samsara. Demi-gods are similar to gods, but their bodies, possessions, and environments are inferior. See *Joyful Path of Good Fortune*.

Dharma Buddha's teachings and the inner realizations that are attained in dependence upon practising them. 'Dharma' means 'protection'. By practising Buddha's teachings, we protect ourself from suffering and problems.

Distraction A deluded mental factor that wanders to any object of delusion.

Dualistic appearance The appearance to mind of an object together with the inherent existence of that object. See *The New Heart of Wisdom*.

Eight Great Sons   The eight principal Mahayana disciples of Buddha Shakyamuni: Avalokiteshvara, Manjushri, Vajrapani, Maitreya, Samantabhadra, Ksitigarbha, Sarvanivaranaviskambini and Akashagarbha. At the time of Buddha, they appeared in the aspect of Bodhisattvas, demonstrating the correct manner of practising the Mahayana paths and helping to spread Buddha's teachings extensively for the benefit of others.

Eight Verses of Training the Mind   Composed by Bodhisattva Langri Tangpa in the eleventh century, this text reveals the essence of the Mahayana Buddhist path to enlightenment. For a translation and full commentary, see *The New Eight Steps to Happiness*.

Eight worldly concerns   The objects of the eight worldly concerns are happiness and suffering, wealth and poverty, praise and criticism, and good reputation and bad reputation. These are called 'worldly concerns' because worldly people are constantly concerned with them, wanting some and trying to avoid others.

Engaging bodhichitta   After we have taken the Bodhisattva vows, our aspiring bodhichitta transforms into engaging bodhichitta, which is a mind that actually engages in the practices that lead to enlightenment.

Enlightenment   Omniscient wisdom whose nature is the permanent cessation of mistaken appearance, and whose function is to bestow mental peace on all living beings. See *Joyful Path of Good Fortune, Mahamudra Tantra* and *Modern Buddhism*.

Extreme of attachment   Also known as 'extreme of samsara', this refers to being attached to the true existence of phenomena, and thus remaining in samsara due to delusion and karma.

Extreme of fear   Also known as 'extreme of solitary peace', this refers to being afraid of the sufferings of samsara, and as a result seeking liberation for oneself alone.

Faith   A naturally virtuous mind that functions mainly to oppose the perception of faults in its observed object. There are three types of faith: believing faith, admiring faith and wishing faith. See *Joyful Path of Good Fortune*, *Modern Buddhism* and *How to Transform Your Life*.

Feeling   A mental factor that functions to experience pleasant, unpleasant or neutral objects. See *How to Understand the Mind*.

Form realm   The environment of the gods who possess form.

Four noble truths   True sufferings, true origins, true cessations and true paths. They are called 'noble' truths because they are supreme objects of meditation. They are sometimes referred to as the 'four truths of Superiors'. Through meditation on the four noble truths, we can realize ultimate truth directly and thus become a noble, or Superior, being. See *How to Solve Our Human Problems* and *Joyful Path of Good Fortune*.

Four opponent powers   Four powers that are essential for successful purification: the power of reliance, the power of regret, the power of the opponent force and the power of promise. See *The Bodhisattva Vow*.

Functioning thing   A phenomenon that is produced and disintegrates within a moment. Synonymous with impermanent phenomenon, thing and product.

God   'Deva' in Sanskrit. A being of the god realm, the highest of the six realms of samsara. There are many different types of god. Some are desire realm gods, while others are form or formless realm gods. See *Joyful Path of Good Fortune*.

Hearer   One of two types of Hinayana practitioner. Both Hearers and Solitary Realizers are Hinayanists, but they differ in their motivation, behaviour, merit, and wisdom. In all these respects, Solitary Realizers are superior to Hearers. See *Ocean of Nectar*.

Hell realm   The lowest of the six realms of samsara. See *Joyful Path of Good Fortune*.

Hinayana   Sanskrit term for 'Lesser Vehicle'. The Hinayana goal is to attain merely one's own liberation from suffering by completely abandoning delusions. See *Joyful Path of Good Fortune*.

Humility   A virtuous mental factor whose main function is to reduce deluded pride. See *The New Eight Steps to Happiness*.

Hungry spirit   A being of the hungry spirit realm, the second lowest of the six realms of samsara. See *Joyful Path of Good Fortune*.

Imputation   According to the Madhyamika-Prasangika school, all phenomena are merely imputed by conception in dependence upon their basis of imputation. Therefore, they are mere imputation and do not exist from their own side. See *The New Heart of Wisdom*.

Inherent existence   An imagined mode of existence whereby phenomena are held to exist from their own side, independent of other phenomena. In reality, all phenomena lack, or are empty of, inherent existence because they depend upon their parts. See *Modern Buddhism* and *The New Heart of Wisdom*.

Ishvara   A god who abides in the Land of Controlling Emanations, the highest state of existence within the desire realm. Ishvara has limited, contaminated miracle powers that make him more powerful than other beings in the desire realm.

Je Tsongkhapa (1357-1419 CE) An emanation of the Wisdom Buddha Manjushri, whose appearance in fourteenth-century Tibet as a monk, and the holder of the lineage of pure view and pure deeds, was prophesied by Buddha. He spread a very pure Buddhadharma throughout Tibet, showing how to combine the practices of Sutra and Tantra, and how to practise pure Dharma during degenerate times. His tradition later became known as the 'Gelug', or 'Ganden Tradition'. See *Heart Jewel* and *Great Treasury of Merit*.

Kadampa A Tibetan word in which 'Ka' means 'word' and refers to all Buddha's teachings, 'dam' refers to Atisha's special Lamrim instructions known as the 'stages of the path to enlightenment', and 'pa' refers to a follower of Kadampa Buddhism who integrates all the teachings of Buddha that they know into their Lamrim practice. See also *Kadampa Buddhism* and *Kadampa Tradition*.

Kadampa Buddhism A Mahayana Buddhist school founded by the great Indian Buddhist Master Atisha (982-1054 CE). See also *Kadampa* and *Kadampa Tradition*.

Kadampa Tradition The pure tradition of Buddhism established by Atisha. Followers of this tradition up to the time of Je Tsongkhapa are known as 'Old Kadampas', and those after the time of Je Tsongkhapa are known as 'New Kadampas'. See also *Kadampa* and *Kadampa Buddhism*. See *Modern Buddhism*.

Karma Sanskrit word meaning 'action'. Through the force of intention, we perform actions with our body, speech and mind, and all of these actions produce effects. The effect of virtuous actions is happiness and the effect of negative actions is suffering. See *Joyful Path of Good Fortune*.

Lamrim   A Tibetan term, literally meaning 'stages of the path'. A special arrangement of all Buddha's teachings that is easy to understand and put into practice. It reveals all the stages of the path to enlightenment. For a full commentary, see *Joyful Path of Good Fortune*.

Langri Tangpa, Bodhisattva   (1054-1123 CE) A great Kadampa Teacher who was famous for his realization of exchanging self with others. He composed *Eight Verses of Training the Mind*. See *The New Eight Steps to Happiness*.

Liberation   'Nirvana' in Sanskrit. Complete freedom from samsara and its cause, the delusions. See *Joyful Path of Good Fortune*.

Living being   Any being who possesses a mind that is contaminated by delusions or their imprints. Both 'living being' and 'sentient being' are terms used to distinguish beings whose minds are contaminated by either of these two obstructions from Buddhas, whose minds are completely free from these obstructions.

Lord of Death   Although the mara, or demon, of uncontrolled death is not a living being, it is personified as the Lord of Death, or 'Yama'. The Lord of Death is depicted in the diagram of the Wheel of Life clutching the wheel between his claws and teeth. See *Joyful Path of Good Fortune*.

Lower realms   The hell realm, hungry spirit realm and animal realm. See also *Samsara*.

Madhyamika   A Sanskrit term, literally meaning 'Middle Way'. The higher of the two schools of Mahayana tenets. The Madhyamika view was taught by Buddha in the *Perfection of Wisdom Sutras* during the second turning of the Wheel of Dharma and was subsequently elucidated by Nagarjuna and his followers. There are two divisions of this school, Madhyamika-Svatantrika and Madhyamika-Prasangika, of which the latter is Buddha's final view. See *Ocean of Nectar*.

Mahayana   Sanskrit term for 'Great Vehicle', the spiritual path to great enlightenment. The Mahayana goal is to attain Buddhahood for the benefit of all living beings by completely abandoning delusions and their imprints. See *Joyful Path of Good Fortune*.

Maitreya   The embodiment of the loving kindness of all the Buddhas. At the time of Buddha Shakyamuni he manifested as a Bodhisattva disciple. In the future, he will manifest as the fifth founding Buddha.

Manjushri   The embodiment of the wisdom of all the Buddhas.

Mantra   A Sanskrit word, literally meaning 'mind protection'. Mantra protects the mind from ordinary appearances and conceptions. There are four types of mantra: mantras that are mind, mantras that are inner wind, mantras that are sound and mantras that are form. In general, there are three types of mantra recitation: verbal recitation, mental recitation and vajra recitation. See *Tantric Grounds and Paths*.

Meditation   Meditation is a mind that concentrates on a virtuous object, and is a mental action that is the main cause of mental peace. There are two types of meditation – analytical meditation and placement meditation. When we use our imagination, mindfulness, and powers of reasoning to find our object of meditation, this is analytical meditation. When we find our object and hold it single-pointedly, this is placement meditation. There are different types of object. Some, such as impermanence or emptiness, are objects apprehended by the mind. Others, such as love, compassion, and renunciation, are actual states of mind. We engage in analytical meditation until the specific object that we seek appears clearly to our mind or until the particular state of mind that we wish to generate arises. This object or state of mind is our object of placement meditation. See *The New Meditation Handbook*.

Mental factor   A cognizer that principally apprehends a particular attribute of an object. Each moment of mind comprises a primary mind and various mental factors. See *How to Understand the Mind*.

Mental stabilization   Generally, the terms 'mental stabilization' and 'concentration' are interchangeable. More specifically, the term 'concentration' is used to refer to the nature of concentration, which is single-pointedness, and the term 'mental stabilization' is used to refer to the function of concentration, which is stability.

Merit   The good fortune created by virtuous actions. It is the potential power to increase our good qualities and produce happiness.

Method practice   Any spiritual path that functions to ripen our Buddha lineage. Training in renunciation, compassion and bodhichitta are examples of method practices.

Mind   That which is clarity and cognizes. Mind is clarity because it always lacks form and because it possesses the actual power to perceive objects. Mind cognizes because its function is to know or perceive objects. See *Clear Light of Bliss*, *How to Understand the Mind* and *Mahamudra Tantra*.

Mindfulness   A mental factor that functions not to forget the object realized by the primary mind. See *How to Understand the Mind*.

Miserliness A deluded mental factor that, motivated by desirous attachment, holds onto things tightly and does not want to part with them. See *How to Understand the Mind*.

Mount Meru According to Buddhist cosmology, a divine mountain that stands at the centre of the universe.

Nagarjuna A great Indian Buddhist scholar and meditation master who revived the Mahayana in the first century CE by bringing to light the teachings on the *Perfection of Wisdom Sutras*. See *Modern Buddhism* and *Ocean of Nectar*.

Negative phenomenon An object that is realized through the mind explicitly eliminating a negated object. There are two types of negative phenomena: affirming negatives and non-affirming negatives. An affirming negative is a negative phenomenon realized by a mind that eliminates its negated object while realizing another phenomenon. A non-affirming negative is a negative phenomenon realized by a mind that merely eliminates its negated object without realizing another phenomenon. See *Ocean of Nectar*.

Non-alertness A deluded mental factor that, being unable to distinguish faults from non-faults, causes us to develop faults.

Non-conscientiousness A deluded mental factor that wishes to engage in non-virtuous actions without restraint.

Non-existent Traditional examples of non-existents are a horn on a rabbit's head and a child of a barren woman. A horn on a rabbit's head, for example, is not established by any valid mind and is consequently a non-existent rather than a conventional (or ultimate) truth. See *The New Heart of Wisdom*.

Object of negation An object explicitly negated by a mind realizing a negative phenomenon. In meditation on emptiness, or lack of inherent existence, it refers to inherent existence. Also known as 'negated object'. See *Modern Buddhism*.

Obstructions to liberation   Obstructions that prevent the attainment of liberation. All delusions, such as ignorance, attachment and anger, together with their seeds, are obstructions to liberation. Also called 'delusion-obstructions'.

Obstructions to omniscience   The imprints of delusions, which prevent simultaneous and direct realization of all phenomena. Only Buddhas have overcome these obstructions. Also called 'obstructions to knowing'.

Patience   A virtuous determination to forbear harm, suffering, or profound Dharma. See *How to Solve Our Human Problems*.

Perfection of Wisdom Sutras   Sutras of the second turning of the Wheel of Dharma, in which Buddha revealed his final view of the ultimate nature of all phenomena – emptiness of inherent existence. See *The New Heart of Wisdom* and *Ocean of Nectar*.

Permanent phenomenon   Phenomena are either permanent or impermanent. A permanent phenomenon is a phenomenon that does not depend upon causes and that does not disintegrate moment by moment.

Prasangika   See *Madhyamika*.

Pretension   A deluded mental factor that, motivated by attachment to wealth or reputation, wishes to pretend that we possess qualities that we do not possess.

Pride   A deluded mental factor that, through considering and exaggerating one's own good qualities or possessions, feels arrogant.

Primary mind A cognizer that principally apprehends the mere entity of an object. Synonymous with consciousness. There are six primary minds: eye consciousness, ear consciousness, nose consciousness, tongue consciousness, body consciousness and mental consciousness. Each moment of mind comprises a primary mind and various mental factors. A primary mind and its accompanying mental factors are the same entity but have different functions. See *How to Understand the Mind*.

Proponents of things The Vaibhashika, Sautrantika and Chittamatra Buddhist schools are known as 'proponents of things' because they assert that things are truly existent. See *Ocean of Nectar*.

Prostration An action of showing respect with body, speech or mind. See *The Bodhisattva Vow*.

Pure Land A pure environment in which there are no true sufferings. There are many Pure Lands. For example, Tushita is the Pure Land of Buddha Maitreya, Sukhavati is the Pure Land of Buddha Amitabha, and Keajra is the Pure Land of Buddha Vajrayogini and Buddha Heruka. See *Living Meaningfully, Dying Joyfully*.

Purification Generally, any practice that leads to the attainment of a pure body, speech or mind. More specifically, a practice for purifying negative karma by means of the four opponent powers. See *The Bodhisattva Vow*.

Refuge Actual protection. To go for refuge to Buddha, Dharma, and Sangha means to have faith in these Three Jewels and to rely upon them for protection from all fears and suffering. See *Joyful Path of Good Fortune*.

Renunciation The wish to be released from samsara. See *Joyful Path of Good Fortune*.

Samantabhadra   Sanskrit name for 'All Good One', a Bodhisattva renowned for his extensive offerings. See *Great Treasury of Merit*.

Samkhya   A non-Buddhist school, the oldest of the Brahmaic schools. See *Ocean of Nectar*.

Samsara   This can be understood in two ways – as uninterrupted rebirth without freedom or control, or as the aggregates of a being who has taken such a rebirth. Samsara, sometimes known as 'cyclic existence', is characterized by suffering and dissatisfaction. There are six realms of samsara. Listed in ascending order according to the type of karma that causes rebirth in them, they are the realms of the hell beings, hungry spirits, animals, human beings, demi-gods and gods. The first three are lower realms or unhappy migrations, and the second three are higher realms or happy migrations. Although from the point of view of the karma that causes rebirth there, the god realm is the highest realm in samsara, the human realm is said to be the most fortunate realm because it provides the best conditions for attaining liberation and enlightenment. See *Joyful Path of Good Fortune*.

Sangha   According to the Vinaya tradition, any community of four or more fully ordained monks or nuns. In general, ordained or lay people who take Bodhisattva vows or Tantric vows can also be said to be Sangha. See *Joyful Path of Good Fortune*.

Self   An I imputed in dependence upon any of the five aggregates. Person, being, self and I are synonyms. See *How to Understand the Mind*.

Self-cherishing   A mental attitude that considers oneself to be supremely important and precious. See *The New Eight Steps to Happiness*.

Self-cognizer   A consciousness that experiences itself.

Self-grasping   A conceptual mind that holds any phenomenon to be inherently existent. The mind of self-grasping gives rise to all other delusions, such as anger and attachment. It is the root cause of all suffering and dissatisfaction. See *The New Heart of Wisdom* and *Modern Buddhism*.

Sense of shame   A mental factor that functions to avoid inappropriate actions for reasons that concern oneself. See *How to Understand the Mind*.

Six perfections   The perfections of giving, moral discipline, patience, effort, mental stabilization and wisdom. They are called 'perfections' because they are motivated by bodhichitta.

Six powers   The five sense powers and the mental power. A sense power is an inner power located in the very centre of a sense organ that functions directly to produce a sense awareness. There are five sense powers, one for each type of sense awareness. A mental power is a mind that principally functions directly to produce the uncommon aspect of a mental awareness. See *How to Understand the Mind*.

Solitary Realizer   One of two types of Hinayana practitioner. See also *Hearer*. See *Ocean of Nectar*.

Spiritual Guide   'Guru' in Sanskrit, 'Lama' in Tibetan. A Teacher who guides us along the spiritual path. See *Joyful Path of Good Fortune* and *Great Treasury of Merit*.

Stupa   A symbolic representation of Buddha's mind.

Sugata   Another Sanskrit term for a Buddha. It indicates that Buddhas have attained a state of immaculate and indestructible bliss.

Sukhavati   Sanskrit term for 'Pure Land of Bliss' or 'Blissful Land' – the Pure Land of Buddha Amitabha.

Superior seeing   A special wisdom that sees its object clearly, and that is maintained by tranquil abiding and the special suppleness that is induced by investigation. See *Joyful Path of Good Fortune*.

Tathagata   Sanskrit term for 'A Being Gone Beyond', which is another term for Buddha.

Ten directions   The four cardinal directions, the four intermediate directions, and the directions above and below.

Three higher trainings   Training in moral discipline, concentration and wisdom motivated by renunciation or bodhichitta.

Three Jewels   The three objects of refuge: Buddha Jewel, Dharma Jewel, and Sangha Jewel. They are called 'Jewels' because they are both rare and precious. See *Joyful Path of Good Fortune*.

Three worlds   In the context of this text, 'worlds' refers to 'realms'. The 'three worlds' are therefore the desire realm, the form realm and the formless realm, which are the three levels within samsara. The desire realm is the environment of hell beings, hungry spirits, animals, human beings, demi-gods and the gods who enjoy the five objects of desire. The form realm is the environment of the gods who possess form. The formless realm is the environment of the gods who do not possess form.

Training the mind   'Lojong' in Tibetan. A special lineage of instructions that came from Buddha Shakyamuni through Manjushri and Shantideva to Atisha and the Kadampa Teachers, which emphasizes the generation of bodhichitta through the practices of equalizing and exchanging self with others combined with taking and giving. See *Universal Compassion* and *The New Eight Steps to Happiness*.

Training the Mind in Seven Points A commentary to *Eight Verses of Training the Mind*, composed by Bodhisattva Chekhawa. For a translation and full commentary, see *Universal Compassion*.

Tranquil abiding A concentration that possesses the special bliss of physical and mental suppleness that is attained in dependence upon completing the nine mental abidings. See *Joyful Path of Good Fortune*.

True existence Existence in any way independent of conceptual imputation.

True-grasping A conceptual mind that apprehends true existence.

Truth Body 'Dharmakaya' in Sanskrit. The Wisdom Truth Body and the Nature Body of a Buddha. The first is Buddha's omniscient mind, and the second is the emptiness, or ultimate nature, of his or her mind. See *Joyful Path of Good Fortune*.

Vaibhashika The lower of the two schools of Hinayana tenets. This school does not accept self-cognizers and asserts external objects to be truly existent. See *Ocean of Nectar*.

Vajrapani The embodiment of the power of all the Buddhas. He appears in a wrathful aspect, displaying his power to overcome outer, inner and secret obstacles. At the time of Buddha Shakyamuni, he manifested as a Bodhisattva disciple.

Valid cognizer A cognizer that is non-deceptive with respect to its engaged object. There are two types: inferential valid cognizers and direct valid cognizers. See *How to Understand the Mind*.

Vow A virtuous determination to abandon particular faults that is generated in conjunction with a traditional ritual. The three sets of vows are the Pratimoksha vows of individual liberation, the Bodhisattva vows, and the Secret Mantra or Tantric vows. See *The Bodhisattva Vow* and *Tantric Grounds and Paths*.

Wishfulfilling jewel A legendary jewel that grants all wishes.

Yogi/Yogini Sanskrit words usually referring to a male or a female meditator who has attained the union of tranquil abiding and superior seeing.

Bibliography

Venerable Geshe Kelsang Gyatso Rinpoche is a highly respected meditation master and scholar of the Mahayana Buddhist tradition founded by Je Tsongkhapa. Since arriving in the West in 1977, Venerable Geshe Kelsang Gyatso Rinpoche has worked tirelessly to establish pure Buddhadharma throughout the world. Over this period he has given extensive teachings on the major scriptures of the Mahayana. These teachings provide a comprehensive presentation of the essential Sutra and Tantra practices of Mahayana Buddhism.

Books

The following books by Venerable Geshe Kelsang Gyatso Rinpoche are all published by Tharpa Publications.

The Bodhisattva Vow A practical guide to helping others. (2nd. edn., 1995)

Clear Light of Bliss A Tantric meditation manual. (3rd. edn., 2014)

Essence of Vajrayana The Highest Yoga Tantra practice of Heruka body mandala. (2nd. edn., 2017)

Great Treasury of Merit How to rely upon a Spiritual Guide. (2nd. edn., 2015)

Guide to the Bodhisattva's Way of Life How to enjoy a life of great meaning and altruism. (A translation of Shantideva's famous verse masterpiece.) (2nd. edn., 2018)

Heart Jewel The essential practices of Kadampa Buddhism. (2nd. edn., 1997)

How to Solve Our Human Problems The four noble truths. (2005)

How to Transform Your Life A blissful journey. (3rd. edn., 2016)

How to Understand the Mind The nature and power of the mind. (4th. edn., 2014)

Introduction to Buddhism An explanation of the Buddhist way of life. (2nd. edn., 2001)

Joyful Path of Good Fortune The path to the supreme happiness of enlightenment. (3rd. edn., 2016)

Living Meaningfully, Dying Joyfully The profound practice of transference of consciousness. (1999)

Mahamudra Tantra The supreme Heart Jewel nectar. (2005)

Meaningful to Behold Becoming a friend of the world. (6th. edn., 2016)

The Mirror of Dharma with Additions How to find the real meaning of human life. (2nd. edn., 2019)

Modern Buddhism The Path of Compassion and Wisdom. (2nd. edn., 2013)

The New Eight Steps to Happiness The Buddhist way of loving kindness. (3rd. edn., 2016)

The New Guide to Dakini Land The Highest Yoga Tantra practice of Buddha Vajrayogini. (3rd. edn., 2012)

The New Heart of Wisdom Profound teachings from Buddha's heart (An explanation of the *Heart Sutra*). (5th. edn., 2012)

The New Meditation Handbook Meditations to make our life happy and meaningful. (5th. edn., 2013)

Ocean of Nectar The true nature of all things. (2nd. edn., 2017)

The Oral Instructions of Mahamudra The very essence of Buddha's teachings of Sutra and Tantra. (2nd. edn., 2016)

Tantric Grounds and Paths How to enter, progress on, and complete the Vajrayana path. (2nd. edn., 2016)

Universal Compassion Inspiring solutions for difficult times. (5th. edn., 2018)

Sadhanas and Other Booklets

Venerable Geshe Kelsang Rinpoche has also supervised the translation of a collection of essential sadhanas, or ritual prayers for spiritual attainments, available in booklet or audio formats.

Avalokiteshvara Sadhana Prayers and requests to the Buddha of Compassion.

The Blissful Path The condensed self-generation sadhana of Vajrayogini.

The Bodhisattva's Confession of Moral Downfalls The purification practice of the *Mahayana Sutra of the Three Superior Heaps*.

Condensed Long Life Practice of Buddha Amitayus.

Dakini Yoga The middling self-generation sadhana of Vajrayogini.

Drop of Essential Nectar A special fasting and purification practice in conjunction with Eleven-faced Avalokiteshvara.

Essence of Good Fortune Prayers for the six preparatory practices for meditation on the stages of the path to enlightenment.

Essence of Vajrayana Heruka body mandala self-generation sadhana according to the system of Mahasiddha Ghantapa.

Feast of Great Bliss Vajrayogini self-initiation sadhana.

Great Liberation of the Father Preliminary prayers for Mahamudra meditation in conjunction with Heruka practice.

Great Liberation of the Mother Preliminary prayers for Mahamudra meditation in conjunction with Vajrayogini practice.

The Great Mother A method to overcome hindrances and obstacles by reciting the *Essence of Wisdom Sutra* (the *Heart Sutra*).

A Handbook for the Daily Practice of Bodhisattva and Tantric Vows.

Heart Jewel The Guru yoga of Je Tsongkhapa combined with the condensed sadhana of his Dharma Protector.

Heartfelt Prayers Funeral service for cremations and burials.

Heruka Body Mandala Burning Offering.

The Hundreds of Deities of the Joyful Land According to Highest Yoga Tantra The Guru Yoga of Je Tsongkhapa as a Preliminary Practice for Mahamudra.

The Kadampa Way of Life The essential practice of Kadam Lamrim.

Keajra Heaven The essential commentary to the practice of *The Uncommon Yoga of Inconceivability*.

Lay Pratimoksha Vow Ceremony.

Liberating Prayer Praise to Buddha Shakyamuni.

Liberation from Sorrow Praises and requests to the Twenty-one Taras.

Mahayana Refuge Ceremony and Bodhisattva Vow Ceremony.

Medicine Buddha Prayer A method for benefiting others.

Medicine Buddha Sadhana A method for accomplishing the attainments of Medicine Buddha.

Meditation and Recitation of Solitary Vajrasattva.

Melodious Drum Victorious in all Directions The extensive fulfilling and restoring ritual of the Dharma Protector, the great king Dorje Shugden, in conjunction with Mahakala, Kalarupa, Kalindewi and other Dharma Protectors.

The New Essence of Vajrayana Heruka body mandala self-generation practice, an instruction of the Ganden Oral Lineage.

Offering to the Spiritual Guide (*Lama Chopa*) A special way of relying upon a Spiritual Guide.

Path of Compassion for the Deceased Powa sadhana for the benefit of the deceased.

Pathway to the Pure Land Training in powa – the transference of consciousness.

Powa Ceremony Transference of consciousness for the deceased.

Prayers for Meditation Brief preparatory prayers for meditation.

Prayers for World Peace.

A Pure Life The practice of taking and keeping the eight Mahayana precepts.

Quick Path to Great Bliss The extensive self-generation sadhana of Vajrayogini.

Request to the Holy Spiritual Guide Venerable Geshe Kelsang Gyatso Rinpoche from his Faithful Disciples.

The Root Tantra of Heruka and Vajrayogini Chapters One & Fifty-one of the *Condensed Heruka Root Tantra*.

The Root Text: Eight Verses of Training the Mind.

Treasury of Wisdom The sadhana of Venerable Manjushri.

The Uncommon Yoga of Inconceivability The special instruction of how to reach the Pure Land of Keajra with this human body.

Union of No More Learning Heruka body mandala self-initiation sadhana.

Vajrayogini Burning Offering.

The Vows and Commitments of Kadampa Buddhism.

Wishfulfilling Jewel The Guru yoga of Je Tsongkhapa combined with the sadhana of his Dharma Protector.

The Yoga of Buddha Amitayus A special method for increasing lifespan, wisdom and merit.

The Yoga of Buddha Heruka The essential self-generation sadhana of Heruka body mandala & Condensed six-session yoga.

The Yoga of Buddha Maitreya Self-generation sadhana.

The Yoga of Buddha Vajrapani Self-generation sadhana.

The Yoga of Enlightened Mother Arya Tara Self-generation sadhana.

The Yoga of Great Mother Prajnaparamita Self-generation sadhana.

The Yoga of Thousand-armed Avalokiteshvara Self-generation sadhana.

The Yoga of White Tara, Buddha of Long Life.

To order any of our publications, or to receive a catalogue, please visit www.tharpa.com or contact your nearest Tharpa Office listed on pages 239-240.

NKT-IKBU

Study Programmes of
Kadampa Buddhism

Kadampa Buddhism is a Mahayana Buddhist school founded by the great Indian Buddhist Master Atisha (982-1054 CE). His followers are known as 'Kadampas'. 'Ka' means 'word' and refers to Buddha's teachings, and 'dam' refers to Atisha's special Lamrim instructions known as 'the stages of the path to enlightenment'. By integrating their knowledge of all Buddha's teachings into their practice of Lamrim, and by integrating this into their everyday lives, Kadampa Buddhists are encouraged to use Buddha's teachings as practical methods for transforming daily activities into the path to enlightenment. The great Kadampa Teachers are famous not only for being great scholars, but also for being spiritual practitioners of immense purity and sincerity.

The lineage of these teachings, both their oral transmission and blessings, was then passed from Teacher to disciple, spreading throughout much of Asia, and now to many countries throughout the world. Buddha's teachings, which are known as 'Dharma', are likened to a wheel that moves from country to country in accordance with changing conditions and people's karmic inclinations. The external forms of presenting Buddhism may change as it meets with different cultures and societies, but its essential authenticity is ensured through the continuation of an unbroken lineage of realized practitioners.

Kadampa Buddhism was first introduced to the modern world in 1977 by the renowned Buddhist Master, Venerable Geshe Kelsang Gyatso Rinpoche. Since that time, he has worked tirelessly to spread Kadampa Buddhism throughout the world by giving extensive teachings, writing many profound texts on Kadampa Buddhism, and founding the New Kadampa Tradition – International Kadampa Buddhist Union (NKT-IKBU), which now has over a thousand Kadampa Buddhist Centres worldwide. Each Centre offers study programmes on Buddhist psychology, philosophy and meditation instruction, as well as retreats for all levels of practitioner. The emphasis is on integrating Buddha's teachings into daily life to solve our human problems and to spread lasting peace and happiness throughout the world.

The Kadampa Buddhism of the NKT-IKBU is an entirely independent Buddhist tradition and has no political affiliations. It is an association of Buddhist Centres and practitioners that derive their inspiration and guidance from the example of the ancient Kadampa Buddhist Masters and their teachings, as presented by Venerable Geshe Kelsang Gyatso Rinpoche.

There are three reasons why we need to study and practise the teachings of Buddha: to develop our wisdom, to cultivate a good heart and to maintain a peaceful state of mind. If we do not strive to develop our wisdom, we will always remain ignorant of ultimate truth – the true nature of reality. Although we wish for happiness, our ignorance leads us to engage in non-virtuous actions, which are the main cause of all our suffering. If we do not cultivate a good heart, our selfish motivation destroys harmony and good relationships with others. We have no peace, and no chance to gain pure happiness. Without inner peace, outer peace is impossible. If we do not maintain a peaceful state of mind, we are not happy even if we have ideal conditions. On the other hand, when our mind is peaceful, we are happy, even if our external conditions are unpleasant. Therefore, the development of these qualities is of utmost importance for our daily happiness.

Venerable Geshe Kelsang Gyatso Rinpoche, or 'Venerable Geshe-la' as he is affectionately called by his students, has designed three special spiritual programmes for the systematic study and practice of Kadampa Buddhism that are especially suited to the modern world – the General Programme (GP), the Foundation Programme (FP) and the Teacher Training Programme (TTP).

GENERAL PROGRAMME

The General Programme provides a basic introduction to Buddhist view, meditation and practice that is suitable for beginners. It also includes advanced teachings and practice from both Sutra and Tantra.

FOUNDATION PROGRAMME

The Foundation Programme provides an opportunity to deepen our understanding and experience of Buddhism through a systematic study of six texts:

1 *Joyful Path of Good Fortune* – a commentary to
   Atisha's Lamrim instructions, the stages of the
   path to enlightenment.
2 *Universal Compassion* – a commentary to
   Bodhisattva Chekhawa's *Training the Mind in Seven
   Points*.
3 *The New Eight Steps to Happiness* – a commentary
   to Bodhisattva Langri Tangpa's *Eight Verses of
   Training the Mind*.
4 *The New Heart of Wisdom* – a commentary to the
   Heart Sutra.
5 *Meaningful to Behold* – a commentary to Venerable
   Shantideva's *Guide to the Bodhisattva's Way of Life*.
6 *How to Understand the Mind* – a detailed
   explanation of the mind, based on the works of the
   Buddhist scholars Dharmakirti and Dignaga.

The benefits of studying and practising these texts are as
follows:

(1) *Joyful Path of Good Fortune* – we gain the ability to put all
Buddha's teachings of both Sutra and Tantra into practice.
We can easily make progress on, and complete, the stages of
the path to the supreme happiness of enlightenment. From a
practical point of view, Lamrim is the main body of Buddha's
teachings, and the other teachings are like its limbs.

(2) and (3) *Universal Compassion* and *The New Eight Steps
to Happiness* – we gain the ability to integrate Buddha's
teachings into our daily life and solve all our human
problems.

(4) *The New Heart of Wisdom* – we gain a realization of the
ultimate nature of reality. By gaining this realization, we can

eliminate the ignorance of self-grasping, which is the root of all our suffering.

(5) *Meaningful to Behold* – we transform our daily activities into the Bodhisattva's way of life, thereby making every moment of our human life meaningful.

(6) *How to Understand the Mind* – we understand the relationship between our mind and its external objects. If we understand that objects depend upon the subjective mind, we can change the way objects appear to us by changing our own mind. Gradually, we will gain the ability to control our mind and in this way solve all our problems.

TEACHER TRAINING PROGRAMME

The Teacher Training Programme is designed for people who wish to train as authentic Dharma Teachers. In addition to completing the study of fourteen texts of Sutra and Tantra, which include the six texts mentioned above, the student is required to observe certain commitments with regard to behaviour and way of life, and to complete a number of meditation retreats.

A Special Teacher Training Programme is also held at Manjushri Kadampa Meditation Centre, Ulverston, England, and can be studied either by attending the classes at the centre or by correspondence. This special meditation and study programme consists of twelve courses based on the books of Venerable Geshe Kelsang Gyatso Rinpoche: *How to Understand the Mind*; *Modern Buddhism*; *The New Heart of Wisdom*; *Tantric Grounds and Paths*; Shantideva's *Guide to the Bodhisattva's Way of Life* and its commentary, *Meaningful to Behold*; *Ocean of Nectar*; *The New Guide to Dakini Land*; *The Oral Instructions of Mahamudra*; *The New Eight Steps to Happiness*;

The Mirror of Dharma with Additions; *Essence of Vajrayana*; and *Joyful Path of Good Fortune*.

All Kadampa Buddhist Centres are open to the public. Every year we celebrate Festivals in the USA and Europe, including two in England, where people gather from around the world to receive special teachings and empowerments and to enjoy a spiritual holiday. Please feel free to visit us at any time!

For further information about NKT-IKBU study programmes or to find your nearest centre, visit www.kadampa.org, or please contact:

NKT-IKBU Central Office
Conishead Priory, Ulverston,
Cumbria LA12 9QQ, UK
Tel: 01229-588533
Email: info@kadampa.org
Website: www.kadampa.org

or

KMC New York
47 Sweeney Road
Glen Spey, NY 12737, USA
Tel: +1 845-856-9000
or 877-523-2672 (toll-free)
Fax: +1 845-856-2110
Email: info@kadampanewyork.org
Website: www.kadampanewyork.org

Tharpa Offices Worldwide

Tharpa books are currently published in English (UK and US), Chinese, French, German, Italian, Japanese, Portuguese and Spanish. Most languages are available from any Tharpa office listed below.

Tharpa UK
Conishead Priory
ULVERSTON
Cumbria,
LA12 9QQ, UK
Tel: +44 (0)1229-588599
Web: tharpa.com/uk
Email: info.uk@tharpa.com

Tharpa US
47 Sweeney Road
GLEN SPEY,
NY 12737, USA
Tel: +1 845-856-5102
Toll-free: 888-741-3475
Fax: +1 845-856-2110
Web: tharpa.com/us
Email: info.us@tharpa.com

Tharpa Asia
1st Floor Causeway Tower,
16-22 Causeway Road,
Causeway Bay,
HONG KONG
Tel: +(852) 2507 2237
Web: tharpa.com/hk-en
Email: info.asia@tharpa.com

Tharpa Australia
25 McCarthy Road,
MONBULK VIC 3793, AU
Tel: +61 (0)3 9756 7203
Web: tharpa.com/au
Email: info.au@tharpa.com

Tharpa Brazil
Rua Artur de Azevedo 1360
Pinheiros, 05404-003,
  SÃO PAULO, SP, BR
Tel: +55 (11) 3476-2328
Web: tharpa.com.br
Email: info.br@tharpa.com

Tharpa Canada (English)
631 Crawford St.,
TORONTO, ON M6G 3K1, CA
Tel: (+1) 416-762-8710
Fax: (+1) 416-762-2267
Web: tharpa.com/ca
Email: info.ca@tharpa.com

Tharpa Canada (Français)
835 Laurier est Montréal, QC,
  H2J 1G2, CA
Tél: (+1) 514-521-1313
Web: tharpa.com/ca-fr
Email: info.ca-fr@tharpa.com

Tharpa Chile
Av. Seminario 589, Providencia,
SANTIAGO, CL
Tel: +56 91297091/+56 22
9935053
Web: tharpa.com/cl
Email: info.cl@tharpa.com

Tharpa Deutschland (Germany)
Chausseestraße 108,
10115 BERLIN, DE
Tel: +49 (030) 430 55 666
Web: tharpa.com/de
Email: info.de@tharpa.com

Tharpa España (Spain)
Calle La Fábrica 8, Majadahonda,
MADRID, 28221, ES
Tel: +34 911 124 914
Web: tharpa.com/es
Email: info.es@tharpa.com

Tharpa France
Château de Segrais
72220 SAINT-MARS-
D'OUTILLÉ, FR
Tél/Fax : ++33 (0)2 43 87 71 02
Web: tharpa.com/fr
Email: info.fr@tharpa.com

Tharpa Japan
KMC TOKYO,
2F Vogue Daikanyama II,
13-4 Daikanyama-cho,
Shibuya-ku, TOKYO,
150-0034, JP
Web: tharpa.jp
Email: info@kadampa.jp

Tharpa México
Enrique Rébsamen Nº 406
Col. Narvate Poniente,
CUIDAD DE MÉXICO,
CDMX, C.P. 03020, MX

Tel & Fax: +52 (55) 56 39 61 80;
Tel: +52 (55) 56 39 61 86
Web: tharpa.com/mx
Email: info.mx@tharpa.com

Tharpa New Zealand
2 Stokes Road, Mount Eden,
AUCKLAND, 1024, NZ
Tel: +64 09 631 5400
DD Mobile: +64 21 583351
Web: tharpa.com/nz
Email: info.nz@tharpa.com

Tharpa Portugal
Rua Moinho do Gato, 5
Várzea de Sintra
SINTRA, 2710-661, PT
Tel: +351 219 231 064
Web: tharpa.pt
Email: info@tharpa.pt

Tharpa Schweiz (Switzerland)
Mirabellenstrasse 1
CH-8048 ZÜRICH, CH
Tel: +41 44 461 36 88
Web: tharpa.com/ch
Email: info.ch@tharpa.com

Tharpa South Africa
26 Menston Rd., Dawncliffe,
Westcliffe, 3629, KZN,
REP. OF SOUTH AFRICA
Tel: +27 31 266 0096
Web: tharpa.com/za
E-mail: info.za@tharpa.com

Tharpa Sverige (Sweden)
c/o KMC Sweden
Upplandsgatan 18, 113 60
Tel: +46 (0) 72 251 4090
Email: info.se@tharpa.com

Index

The letter 'g' indicates an entry in the glossary

reasons for benefits 9
types 8, 37. *See also*
engaging bodhichitta
Bodhisattva 7, 33, 136, 161, g
object of praise 10–11
obstructing 38
Bodhisattva downfalls 38, 39
Bodhisattva's way of life
viii, 63, 65–67, 102, 156
Bodhisattva vow 39, 67, 80.
See also vow
taking 32–33
bodily conduct 55, 57, 61,
63–64
body 53, 78, 80. *See also*
attachment, to body
abandoning attachment to
59–61, 122, 148–149
boat-like 61, 101
cherishing 139
dream-like 174
essenceless 60
giving 31, 63, 102, 103
impermanence of 40, 122
impure 7, 60, 124–128, 154
offering 16, 23
parts of 172–173
truly-existent 172
Brahma 9, g
Brahmin 161
Buddha 6, 65, 121, 156, g
beseeching to remain 30
countless 39
doctor 24, 103, 163

form of 7, 161
good qualities of 54, 91, 140
illusion-like 155, 162
lineage of 33
nature of living beings 94
Navigator 7
no conceptual mind 161–162
omniscient 54, 63
pleasing 93
quotations of 11, 50, 52, 91,
106, 157
rarity of 39, 190
refuge in 23, 105
repaying kindness of 92–94
requesting to teach 30
teachings of. *See also*
teachings, of Buddha
Buddhahood. *See*
enlightenment
burial ground 122, 128, 130

C

cause and effect 155–156,
181–188, 182, 185. *See also*
karma
illusion-like 76, 187
cessation 188–190
chakravatin king 95–97, g
Chekhawa, Bodhisattva vi, g
cherishing others vi, 62,
92, 137, 139–141. *See also*
equalizing self and
others; exchanging self
with others

reliance, power of 22–23, 65
reliquary 161
remaining as impassive as
  wood 55, 57
renunciation 73, 118, g
reputation 87–88, 121, 188
  losing 53
respect 54, 56, 58, 85

S

Samantabhadra 17, 18, 23,
  198, g. *See also* eight Great
  Sons
Samkhyas g
  refutation of 167–169,
    181–186
samsara 39, 43, 73, 74, 118,
  131, 159, g
  abodes of 165
  conventionally existent 156
  lacks true existence 188
  sufferings of 99, 189
Sangha 105, 203, g
seed and sprout 180, 186
self g
  continuum of 170
  illusion-like 58
  material 169–170
  merely imputed 170
  permanent 75–76,
    167–171, 181
  truly existent 166
  unfindable 171

self-cherishing vii, 77, 133, g
  abandoning 139–141,
    145–151
  faults of 137, 139–141, 144,
    148
  fearful spirit 141
self-cognizer 157–158, g
self-confidence 107–110
self-grasping vii, 159, 192, g.
  See also grasping at true
  existence
  abandoning 122, 135, 171
  of body 60, 139
  of self 137–138, 149
self-important view 57, 108,
  109
selflessness of persons
  166–171, 176, 177
selflessness of phenomena
  171–176
sense awareness 178
sense of shame 54, 58, g
sense power 175. *See also* six
  powers
servant 16, 60, 93, 146
sexual partner 77, 124–131
Shantideva vi
sickness 40, 53, 73, 74, 139,
  190
six perfections 50, 63, 107, g.
  See also individual ones
six powers 175, 177, g
skill 63
slander 80

Further Reading

If you have enjoyed reading this book and would like to find out more about Buddhist thought and practice, here are some books by Venerable Geshe Kelsang Gyatso Rinpoche that you might like to read. They are all available from Tharpa Publications.

A Complete Commentary to
Guide to the Bodhisattva's Way of Life

MEANINGFUL TO BEHOLD
Becoming a Friend of the World

Many people have the compassionate wish to benefit others, but few understand how to accomplish this effectively in daily life. Bodhisattvas are friends of the world who have such strong compassion they are able to transform all their daily activities into a means to benefit others.

The path of the Bodhisattvas was exquisitely explained in the universally loved poem *Guide to the Bodhisattva's Way of Life*. With this commentary the full effectiveness and profundity of this wonderful poem are revealed in full and made applicable for our time.

Also available as an eBook.

MODERN BUDDHISM
The Path of Compassion and Wisdom

Modern Buddhism is a special presentation of Buddha's teachings on compassion and wisdom that communicates their essence in a way that is easy to understand and put into practice.

By developing and maintaining compassion and wisdom in daily life, we can transform our lives, improve our relationships with others and look behind appearances to see the way things actually exist. In this way we can solve all our daily problems and accomplish the real meaning of our human life. With compassion and wisdom, like the two wings of a bird, we can quickly reach the enlightened world of a Buddha. Also available as an audio book.

For a free eBook or PDF of *Modern Buddhism* please see www.emodernbuddhism.com.

HOW TO TRANSFORM YOUR LIFE
A Blissful Journey

A practical manual for daily life that shows how we can develop and maintain inner peace, how we can reduce and stop our experience of problems, and how we can bring about positive changes in our lives that will enable us to experience deep and lasting happiness. This is a significantly revised edition of one of Venerable Geshe Kelsang's most popular and accessible books. Also available as an audio book.

For a free eBook of *How to Transform Your Life* please visit www.howtotyl.com.

UNIVERSAL COMPASSION
Inspiring Solutions for Difficult Times

The heart of Buddha's teachings is unconditional love and compassion. This inspiring explanation of the popular Buddhist poem, *Training the Mind in Seven Points*, reveals powerful and far-reaching methods for us to develop these altruistic states. Ancient meditative techniques that have been tried and tested for centuries are brought alive and made relevant to our everyday experiences.

Also available as an audio book and eBook.

'It could be read with profit by anyone whose religion demands the exercise of compassion.' *Faith and Freedom*.

THE NEW HEART OF WISDOM
Profound Teachings from Buddha's Heart
An Explanation of the *Heart Sutra*

This completely new presentation offers truly liberating insights and advice for the contemporary reader. It reveals the profound meaning of the very heart of Buddha's teachings – the *Perfection of Wisdom Sutras*. The author shows how all our problems and suffering come from our ignorance of the ultimate nature of things and how we abandon this ignorance and come to enjoy pure, lasting happiness through a special wisdom associated with compassion for all living beings.

Also available as an eBook.

'... both excellent and comprehensive.' *North American Board for East West Dialogue*.

'An excellent book ... for the serious student of Buddhism a better book would be hard to come across.' *The Middle Way*.

THE BODHISATTVA VOW
A Practical Guide to Helping Others

How to engage in the essential practices of Mahayana Buddhism by taking and keeping the Bodhisattva vows – practical guidelines for compassionate living – including a purification practice based on the *Sutra of the Three Superior Heaps*. With this handbook as our companion, we can enter the Bodhisattva's way of life and progress with confidence along the path to full enlightenment.

Also available as an audio book and eBook.

HOW TO UNDERSTAND THE MIND
The Nature and Power of the Mind

This book offers us deep insight into our mind, and shows how an understanding of its nature and functions can be used practically in everyday experience to improve our lives.

The first part is a practical guide to developing and maintaining a light, positive mind – showing how to recognize and abandon states of mind that harm us, and to replace them with peaceful and beneficial ones.

The second part describes different types of mind in detail, revealing the depth and profundity of the Buddhist understanding of the mind. It concludes with a detailed explanation of meditation, showing how by controlling and transforming our mind we can attain a lasting state of joy, independent of external conditions.

Also available as an audio book and eBook.

THE NEW EIGHT STEPS TO HAPPINESS
The Buddhist Way of Loving Kindness

This inspiring book explains how to transform all life's difficulties into valuable spiritual insights, by meditating on one of Buddhism's best-loved teachings, *Eight Verses of Training the Mind*, by the great Tibetan Bodhisattva Geshe Langri Tangpa. This ancient wisdom is now available for those seeking lasting happiness and greater meaning in their lives.

Also available as an audio book and eBook.

'... induces calmness and compassion into one's being.' *The New Humanity Journal*.

JOYFUL PATH OF GOOD FORTUNE
The Path to the Supreme Happiness of Enlightenment

We all have the potential for self-transformation, and a limitless capacity for the growth of good qualities, but to fulfil this potential we need to know what to do at every stage of our spiritual journey.

This book offers a detailed explanation of the entire path to enlightenment, with the teachings of Buddha laid out step-by-step making them very easy for the modern reader to put into practice. A perfect guidebook to the Buddhist path.

Also available as an audio book and eBook.

'This book is invaluable.' *World Religions in Education*.

THE NEW MEDITATION HANDBOOK
Meditations to make our life happy and meaningful

This popular and practical manual allows us to discover for ourselves the inner peace and lightness of mind that comes from meditation. The author explains twenty-one step-by-step meditations that lead to increasingly beneficial states of mind, and that together form the entire Buddhist path to enlightenment.

Also available as an audio book and eBook.

'This manual provides a succinct and inspiring overview of the many ways in which Buddhism can be applied to the situations and activities of daily life.' *Spirituality and Health.*

HOW TO SOLVE OUR HUMAN PROBLEMS
The Four Noble Truths

This book shows how Buddha's popular teaching on the Four Noble Truths can help us to solve basic human problems such as dissatisfaction and anger, and provides a profound illumination of our human experience and our potential for deep inner freedom.

Also available as an audio book and eBook.

'This book offers peace of mind in these troubled times.' *Publishing News.*

'Geshe Kelsang Gyatso has a unique gift for addressing everyday difficulties.' *Booklist.*

OCEAN OF NECTAR
The True Nature of All Things

Ocean of Nectar is the first complete explanation in English of Chandrakirti's *Guide to the Middle Way*, a classic Mahayana scripture, which to this day is regarded as the principal presentation of Buddha's profound view of emptiness, the ultimate nature of reality.

With a new translation and verse-by-verse commentary, the author reveals this profound meaning with utmost clarity, and guides us along the stages of the Bodhisattva path to full enlightenment. This book is an indispensable guide for the serious practitioner of Mahayana Buddhism.

Also available as an eBook.

To order any of our publications, or to request a catalogue, please visit www.tharpa.com or contact your nearest Tharpa office listed on pages 239-240.

Finding Your Nearest Kadampa Meditation Centre

To deepen your understanding of this book, and other books published by Tharpa Publications, and its application to everyday life you can receive support and inspiration from qualified Teachers and practitioners.

Tharpa Publications is part of the wider spiritual community of the New Kadampa Tradition. This tradition has a growing number of centres and branches in over 40 countries around the world. All centres and their branches offer study and meditation classes based on this book, and other books on modern Buddhism and meditation, taught by qualified Teachers. For more details, see *Study Programmes of Kadampa Buddhism* (see pages 233-238).

These programmes are based on the study of books by Venerable Geshe Kelsang Gyatso Rinpoche and are designed to fit comfortably with a modern way of life.

To find your local Kadampa centre
visit: tharpa.com/centres